Why Not Me?

ALSO BY MINDY KALING

Is Everyone Hanging Out Without Me? (And Other Concerns)

Why Not Me?

Mindy Kaling

EBURY
PRESS

7 9 10 8 6

Ebury Press, an imprint of Ebury Publishing
20 Vauxhall Bridge Road
London SW1V 2SA

Ebury Press is part of the Penguin Random House group of companies
whose addresses can be found at global.penguinrandomhouse.com

Penguin
Random House
UK

Book design by Elizabeth Rendfleisch

Endpaper design and interior illustrations by Kate Harmer

In some instances, names and identifying characteristics have
been withheld or changed to protect the privacy of individuals.
Conversations in the book are written from the author's memory.

Mindy Kaling has asserted her right to be identified as the author of this
Work in accordance with the Copyright, Designs and Patents Act 1988

First published by Ebury Press in 2015

First published in the United States by Crown Archetype, an imprint of
Crown Publishing Group, a division of Penguin Random House in 2015

www.eburypublishing.co.uk

A CIP catalogue record for this book is available from the British Library

ISBN 9780091960308

Printed and bound in Great Britain by Clays Ltd, St Ives PLC

For my mother

CONTENTS

HELLO AGAIN

IN SEVENTH GRADE I STARTED AT A NEW school. On the first day, I was so anxious to make friends, I brought a family-size bag of Skittles to homeroom so I could pass them out and entice my new classmates to talk to me. "Do you like Skittles?" I asked. Kids would nod, cautiously. "Here, take some. I'm Mindy!" I said, trying to rope them into conversation. It didn't work very well. Even back then the kids thought this was suspicious behavior, like I was covering for something unseemly they couldn't quite pinpoint. Still, I persisted, striking up conversations like a middle school Hare Krishna, and cornering kids with aggressively banal chitchat. "That's so funny you like the color blue. I like turquoise. *We're so similar.*" I did this until my art teacher, Mr. Posner, pulled me aside.

Mr. Posner was soft-spoken and wouldn't let us talk about the movie *Silence of the Lambs,* because it contained violence against women. I hated him. "You don't have to give people candy to like you, Mindy," he said. "They will like you . . . for *you.*" I nodded meaningfully, knowing he wanted to see that my mind had been blown by his awesome humanity. Then he took my Skittles and I thought, What a load of garbage. At twelve years old, I had experienced enough to have zero faith in the power of my looks or personality to reel in the friends I wanted so badly. I needed my Skittles. The next day I brought in more, and Mr. Posner called my parents. The Skittles stopped, and I wished that Mr. Posner was trapped in the bottom of a well, and later killed, like in *Silence of the Lambs*. My parents encouraged me to play field hockey, where I eventually did end up making a few friends. I remember that time as one of the most stressful periods of my life. Every kid wants approval, but my desire to be well liked was central to my personality.

As I got older, I got craftier and less obvious, but I've always put a lot of energy and effort into people liking me. That's why I've never understood the compliment "effortless." People love to say: "She just walked into the party, charming people with her effortless beauty." I don't understand that at all. What's so wrong with effort, anyway? It means you care. What about the girl who "walked into the party, her determination to please apparent on her eager face"? Sure, she might seem a little crazy, and, yes, maybe everything she says sounds like conversation starters she found on a website, but at least she's trying. Let's give *her* a shot!

And these days, I find I'm caring less and less about what people think of me. Maybe it's my age, maybe it's my security in my career, maybe it's because I'm skrilla flush with that dollah-dollah-bill-y'all, but if I had to identify my overall feeling these days, it's much more "Eh, screw it. Here's how I really feel." The truth is, it's hard to get people to like you, but it's even harder to keep people liking you. You'd have to bring in Skittles every single day. The result of my not caring so much about what I say allows me to care more about *how* I say it. I think it makes my writing more personal and more enjoyable.

If you're reading this, you're probably a woman. Or perhaps you're a gay man getting a present for your even gayer friend. Maybe you accidentally bought this thinking it was the *Malala* book. However this book made its way from the "Female Humor/ Brave Minority Voices/Stress-free Summer Reads!" section of your bookstore to your hands, it doesn't matter. The important thing is you are here now. Welcome. I'm excited to share my stories with you, so you can see what I'm really like. If my childhood, teens, and twenties were about wanting people to like me, now I want people to know me. So, this is a start.

Enjoy.

Mindy Kaling
Los Angeles, California

·· ❧ For the Ladies ❧ ··

HOW TO LOOK SPECTACULAR:
A STARLET'S CONFESSIONS

ოუი

A T SOME POINT IN THE PAST FEW YEARS, I transformed from Mindy Kaling, boring anonymous comedy writer who buys her bras at T.J.Maxx, to this person:

Mindy Kaling, red-carpet glamourpuss with perfect skin and shiny hair, outfitted in the latest fashion garments! Look at me, just lounging on a chair like "I'm so fancy, my torso doesn't even bend!"

Here I am again!

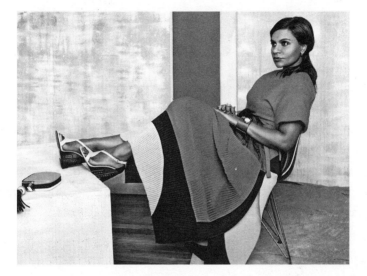

I am telling you, the key to looking gorgeous is to never sit up straight. It implies you have not eaten enough to have the strength to sit like a regular person, which historically is sexy to everyone.

The person above is the creation of a handful of talented people whose job it is to make me look good. I'm of course talking about the hair, makeup, costume, lighting, spackling, and hoisting departments. They all work hard, so all I have to do is show up in my sweatpants and zit cream and say the magic words: "Make me look gorgeous or you're fired."

I'm just kidding! I don't do that. In fact, I don't have to do anything. That's why I'm ~~a starlet~~ extremely grateful. Curious what I looked like before all these people worked their magic on me?

Quite a transformation, huh?

Now, usually, people privy to this kind of valuable information keep it to themselves, because an unspoken rule among actresses is: never tell any other woman the secrets of your beauty, even if she's a ninety-five-year-old background actor playing a cadaver. "Today she's a cadaver; tomorrow she's a cadaver on a CBS drama trying to balance a love life and her demanding job as a district attorney," you think suspiciously. That's why when actresses are asked in interviews about their obvious, face-altering plastic surgery, they say things like "Oh, I would *never* get any work done. Then how do I look like this? I'm just getting a lot of rest, meditating, and staying hydrated." One of the great things about women's magazines is that they accept that drinking water and sitting quietly will make your breasts huge and lips plump up to the size of two bratwursts.

Maybe it's because I'm such a rule breaker, maybe it's because I'm so down-to-earth, or maybe it's because you spent money on this book and I don't want you to return it, but I have decided to share my beauty secrets with you.

Now you too can go from looking like Gollum in *Lord of the Rings* to looking like a sexy, authentic Hollywood lady. Just read all the tricks I've learned and incorporate them into your own routine. It's easy, my precious!

GET YOUR HAIR ON *FLEEK*
(IS THIS WORD STILL COOL? WAS IT EVER?)

The first thing you need to know is that the hair on your head is worthless. The color, the length, the thickness, everything. You will never see anyone on TV sporting their own God-given hair, unless it's on, like, a sad miniseries about factory workers in East Germany.

The same goes for hair color. Yes, your natural color may be appropriate for your skin tone, but this isn't the land of appropriate—*this is Hollywood, baby.* Out here, a dark-skinned woman's traditional hair color is honey blond. A hip white woman's natural hair is gray-lavender.

The real trick to having gorgeous hair is quantity. Piles of thick, cascading, My Little Pony–style hair signifies youth, so if you don't have that, you are basically announcing that you are old and dying. To keep up with the trend, everyone has used hair extensions. And I mean *everyone*. The stenographer who doesn't speak in that judge show you watch. The Long Island Medium. Clooney. Castle. EVERYBODY on the *Today* show, but no one in the Orange Room. The entire family getting a new house on *Extreme Home Makeover*, including the kids. Charlie Rose. The obese woman on *My 600-lb Life*. There are fabled stories of what exactly is on Jeremy Piven's head. I'm not throwing shade. I would look like the Crypt Keeper if you saw me with my natural hair on TV. It's a volume game, and he or she with the most hair wins.

This is how you know you have enough hair:

- The weight of it gives you a splitting headache
- At the end of the day you find stuff in it, like receipts and wet Tic Tacs

- If you are topless, your long and thick hair easily covers both of your breasts, which is great if you have to run to CVS and all of your tops are in the wash
- Hair is always getting caught in your armpits
- You can pull guests up to the window of your second-story apartment with your hair, Rapunzel-style

You're probably wondering where all this hair is coming from. Remember in middle school history class, when you learned about the Dutch East India Company? They would travel all over Asia and India for spices to ship on the spice route to the New World. That mercantile route is essentially the same geographical route hair travels to get to actresses in Los Angeles. Locks of hair are culled from women in Asia and India, but instead of from the Dutch East India Company, you get them from places in downtown Los Angeles with names like *Divastyles Human Hair by Giovanná*.

If you think about where your hair came from for too long, it can be very sad. So I prefer to tell myself vague lies. Like, maybe these are all deeply spiritual women and cutting their hair off is part of some beautiful religious ritual, so they were going to do it anyway, and now they're just getting paid for it; which is better than the reality that these women are all Fantine and we are monsters stealing their hair.

You're probably wondering what you should do with the hair once you have it. I wear colorful, complicated clothes, so I keep my hair and makeup really simple.

If I wear a neon-yellow coat over a checkerboard dress and also have heavy eye shadow and Orphan Annie curls, I will look like your aunt who just came out during Pride Weekend. I have to pick my appearance battles. If you're Natalie Dormer, you can take big fashion risks and shave half your head, and it looks good. If you're a normal person and you try that, you just look like you had recent brain surgery.

SPRAY TANS!
(SURPRISE! I'VE BEEN WHITE ALL ALONG!)

Two or three times a year I get a spray tan. "But why?" you ask. "You already have dark skin. Like, *really* dark skin." Well, first of all, that's a little racially weird that you said that. Second, it's not about changing the color, it's about *evening out* the color. When I wear a strapless dress or act in a nude scene, I have noticeable tan lines just like white people. And unless I've been hired to do an American Apparel thong campaign, which, by the way, I'm totally into doing, tan lines are no bueno for me. So the night before we are shooting a scene where I have to show a lot of skin (which happens way more than I ever thought), I get a spray tan. Basically what that means is a really brave woman named Jen will show up at my house with a machine that looks like a small stainless-steel box to store a gremlin, and I will strip naked and stand in my bathroom with my arms and legs wide open and a guilty expression on my face. You don't have to wear underwear, but I always wear mine because it's important for Jen to know that I am classy. When sweet, patient Jen has finished spraying a temporary dye all over my body with a little airbrush, she uses a blow dryer to dry me off.

I'm so mortified during this entire process that I find relief in relentless chatter. "Oh, I've heard *American Horror Story* is groundbreaking. Tell me all about it! Like, every scene from every episode!" I get really focused on what we are chatting about so, in my mind, it seems like *our conversation* is the reason she is there, not because she needed to paint my boobs with a dye called "Chocolate Mama."

But it's all worth it, because the next day I am a scrumptious, golden-brown delight, like a McDonald's hash brown.

OH, THIS OLD (PERFECTLY TAILORED) THING?

I've always loved clothes. Like any normal woman, I would see a dress, buy it, rip the tags off with my teeth, save the buttons for ten to twelve years in a drawer, and wear it to work. If I was going on a date, I might take a little extra care and use nail clippers to remove the tag, wear a cardigan on top, and cinch the whole look together with a wide belt. "Cinch together the whole look with a wide belt" was a very popular style in the early 2000s, which we believed accentuated our curves but in reality made a generation of women look like we were wearing lumbar support braces.

When I first met my costume designer, Salvador Perez, he was shooting the Lindsay Lohan–starring TV movie *Liz & Dick*, which, from all accounts, was far more tumultuous than any actual interaction Elizabeth Taylor and Richard Burton ever had. The experience was hard on Sal but excellent for me. Sal was so traumatized that he was extra willing to work on a show whose lead actress was only a little bit psychotic.

Sal is a genius and he has taught me that *fit is everything*. Whether it's Gucci or the Gap, he has everything tailored perfectly to my body. And it makes sense, if you think about it. Why should the tunic that looks perfect on the lithe Amazon with the three-foot-long torso modeling it in the J.Crew catalogue look like a bathrobe on me? Oh, because that's what you think I look like? Never mind. Skip this chapter.

People sometimes sweetly say that I have "child-bearing hips," but what they really mean is that I have hips that will definitely knock over your drink if you are sitting next to me on a plane and I have to get up to use the bathroom. I am somewhat happy with my legs, but I often find that when I buy a size up on a skirt to fit over my hips, the skirt becomes a little too long and I look like a religious woman (which I would love, by the way! The doting Jewish husband! The house in Hancock Park! The wigs!). After Sal got me into tailoring, I took all my skirts to get shortened to a much more flattering length. So at least my legs look good when my hips knock your Sprite into your lap.

We needed two people to dress me in a sari, which billions of Indian women put on every day by themselves.

What this means is introducing a tailor into your life. I know what you're thinking: Oh God, not another person I have to interact with. But trust me, this one will be worth it. Your tailor will transform all of your clothes and make them seem new again. Your tailor is the one person who always makes you look better after you see them. Soon you will want to bring them on vacation with you. The best part is now you are one of those people "who has a tailor," which makes you seem really old-fashioned and menacing, like Al Capone. The key to maximizing this perception is making sure you make lots of angry and tense phone calls while your clothes are being measured. When I want to save money, I don't waste my time getting clothes that don't fit from Bloomingdale's; I buy things from a vintage store or an affordable chain and have them tailored to my body type. I wore a tailored dress from Old Navy to a wedding last summer and I was a hit. It couldn't have been my personality; I was drunk as hell that night.

ROBOTS THAT ENHANCE YOUR LOOKS

Ask any Hollywood makeup artist and they will tell you that they would rather cover up a giant green shamrock tattoo that spans half your face, Mike Tyson–style, than a whitehead in the center of your forehead (coincidentally, I have both). The reason is that color is much easier to cover up than dimension. It's way easier to paint over a tattoo than to somehow disguise a protruding pimple.

When we are filming the show, I do not have weeks to wait to get rid of my pimples. It doesn't help that we shoot in high-definition, which means that when the camera is on me in a close-up you can all but count the pores on my nose. By the way, what is our fixation on "high definition" anyway? Everything is HD this and HD that. What if I don't *want* to see things that clearly on my television? Leave something to my imagination, bros. I liked it much better before, when televisions weren't so crystal clear. Like when I was four, watching gymnastics in the 1984 Olympics, and the only way I knew that that red-white-and-blue blur bouncing around on the mat was Mary Lou Retton was because the announcer said so. This is the new cause that I feel most strongly about in my life.

So I have had to learn some drastic ways to get rid of my zits. Only one thing has ever worked, and I have come to depend on one device, a special wand the size and weight of a remote control that shoots hot blue light into my skin.

I bought this wand, the Tria Acne Clearing Blue Light, from my dermatologist's office. At one point I was spending so much time with the device that I started calling him Wall-E. He looks like a fancy sex toy from Japan. His job is to "eliminate acne-causing bacteria deep beneath the skin's surface," and I have to hold him pressed against my face for twenty minutes every night. The little whirring sound he makes when I switch him on is comforting.

And what does Wall-E feel like? Like a tiny white-hot iron you are pressing against an already-sensitive pimple. It's hellish. But it's very effective at squashing and destroying pimples, so you don't care. Also, I think I have a pretty high pain threshold, because one time, after a very long day of shooting, I was using Wall-E while I was watching TV and fell asleep. When I woke up, I had a rectangular burn mark on the side of my chin. But no zits underneath!

YOUR BOOBS MUST BE ON *FLEEK*. (OK, NOW I KNOW IT'S NOT COOL. I'M SAYING IT AS A JOKE.)

I have never had any breasts to speak of. In high school I wore the same white cotton Jockey 34-A bra for three consecutive years. It wasn't that I didn't have other bras; it's just that I barely needed one anyway, and it was comfortable. I did this until one day in the locker room after field-hockey practice, Annie Devereaux asked me in a worried (secretly bitchy) tone, "Why do you only have one bra?" I lied and said I had several exquisite bras at home but I read that underwires give you breast cancer, so I never wore them. Annie was dubious, but the conversation had taken such a depressing turn that she let it go.

Soon after, I made my mom take me to Victoria's Secret, and I saw what I was missing out on. I didn't have to wear my stretchy white bra that looked like it was for someone going through physical therapy. My bra could be fun, sexy, and an outrageous color, like neon-pink. And that wasn't all; they had thongs that had your astrological sign in little crystals over the pubis! Underwear didn't have to be utilitarian; it could be a topic of conversation that

announced your whole deal. My mom was supportive of this because I think she knew there was little to no chance any boy would
ever see them anyway, so hey, why not? I asked her why she never
wore underwear like this. She smiled and said kindly, "These
aren't for serious people." I think she was right, because I have
been wearing crazy bras ever since.

For events, I wear a moderately padded bra. I've found that a well-
fitting padded bra can transform me from a pear-shaped woman to
an hourglass-shaped woman. Okay, maybe not hourglass-shaped,
but definitely, say, an egg-timer-shaped woman. For me, it's not
about being busty; it's about evening out the proportions of my
body. The reason I only wear them to events and not in my every-
day life is that a padded bra can look a little *excessive* on me. One
time I wore one to work when my regular bras were in the wash,
and my friend and coworker Ike Barinholtz stopped in his tracks.
"I'm sorry, why are your boobs so big?!" he asked in a legitimately
concerned tone. This reaction was so much more offensive to me
than if he had said, "Hubba-hubba." I suppose my modest-size
breasts are a constant that the people I work with have come to
depend on. So, I will keep them that way.

LEARN TO LURK IN SHADOWS

Who is the beauty icon that inspires you the most? Is it Sophia
Loren? Audrey Hepburn? Halle Berry? Mine is Nosferatu, because
that vampire taught me my number-one and number-two favorite
beauty tricks of all time: avoid the sun at all costs and always try to
appear shrouded in shadows.

Lighting in television and film is the real key to always looking
beautiful. It's also the biggest mystery to me. I hired my cinematographer, Marco Fargnoli, based on one thing and one thing alone:
his impressive and serious-sounding Italian name. As luck would

have it, he also turned out to be a very talented DP, which means director of photography. Marco can take a foot-long square of orange cellophane—the kind they wrap cookies in at the bakery—and tape it in front of a light, and somehow I go from looking like Ving Rhames to Freida Pinto. It's remarkable. In addition to his other feats (making the San Fernando Valley look like the West Village in Manhattan), he regularly makes me look like this:

Eavesdropping, the most alluring way to be nosy

I can always count on Marco to make me look luminous and adorable, like that kid who is fishing from the moon in the Dream-Works logo. So my advice to you is: try to befriend a cinematographer and have him or her light you wherever you go.

SCARY MASKS!

When I was fifteen, I would wake up, wash my face with the same bar of Lever 2000 I used on my body, wash my hair with an all-in-one shampoo, and be done with it. Back then, we all thought Lever 2000 was the best because the number "2000" seemed so impressive. Were there 1999 formulas before they landed on this one? That sounds really well researched. I'm in!

Oh, how I miss that charmingly low-maintenance version of

myself. Now when I wake up, if I haven't gotten enough sleep, it shows. You know how on *The Walking Dead* when a human gets bitten by a zombie, there's that fifteen-minute window after they are infected when they are transforming into a zombie, and their insides liquefy and their eyes turn into milky goo? That's what I look like.

But no one in America will ever know that, because on those bad-sleep days, my makeup artist Cindy applies a beauty mask to my face. It can be any calming mask. I keep mine in the fridge, because there are two things Mindy Kaling likes cold: beer and beauty masks.* The mask also makes me look like Hannibal Lecter, but at least he was a human, after all. After the potions from the mask seep into my skin, Cindy peels it off and I look like a woman you might want to be friends with. At least acquaintances with. Or at least a woman Michonne wouldn't stab in the brain with her katana.

You can't hear me, but I'm muttering, "You're next."

ARMS ARE NOT YOUR FRIENDS

The most valuable thing I learned from Kim Kardashian is that your arm must never lie flat against your body. The second most

....
* I'm testing out a persona. Is she cool?

valuable thing is how to do this sex move called the Armenian Strangler, but that's for another book. I remember hearing her say that when you put your hand on your hip, it makes your arm look thinner and draws attention to your waist. I tried it and I loved it! So I started doing it whenever I was getting my picture taken.

I guess I was doing it a lot, because a blogger decided to write about it. This blogger had been semiregularly writing mean stuff about me, and this snarky post was called "Mindy Kaling Sure Likes to Pose with Her Hand on Her Hip." The post contained a bunch of photos of me from separate red-carpet events with my hand on my hip. When I first saw it, I felt so bad and embarrassed. What does this observation mean about me? It must mean I'm vapid or, like, really lame or aspirational or something.

Then I realized it meant absolutely nothing at all. This person was desperate for a new way to dis me, and when he (that's right, *he*, men can be catty mean-os too!) couldn't find anything substantive, he chose this, because he figured, well, people probably resent actresses anyway for getting to get dressed up and pose for photos, so readers will love to mock her for this.

And then I thought, Wow, this poor sad guy. I pictured all the time he must have spent scouring through photos of me to find the ones where my hand was on my hip. And when he spotted one, Eureka!, he thought, excitedly dragging the image to his desktop while his wife was probably in another room, watching TV by herself, wondering when he was going to come out of the den. Why doesn't he ever have time for me, she thinks. Next time my boss asks me to get happy-hour hurricanes with him, I'm going to say yes! This was a *grown man*. And that was his *job*. Which brings me to another thing I learned from Kim Kardashian: haters are just more people paying attention to you. And guess what? I looked great in all those photos he compiled.

There, I've spilled all my beauty secrets and it feels really good.

Like, benevolent even? Maybe I will count this as my charity thing for the year. If you found this helpful, then great, and I am more than a little bit surprised. If this all sounded ridiculous and you are laughing at what an idiot I am, that too is great. Because talking about looks isn't important. It's just supposed to be fun.

SOME THOUGHTS ON WEDDINGS

HAVE BEEN LARGELY SILENT ABOUT MY attitude toward weddings. Anyone who knows me even slightly will recognize how unusual that is, since I am notorious for making impassioned speeches about things nobody cares about. Like, I think it's a federal crime parking meters won't accept pennies. Yeah, government, we know pennies suck. But *you* made them! You have to accept them! Parking meters are literally one of the three things anyone uses coins for and you decide you don't want to deal with them?

OK, I took a couple hours off to cool off and now I'm back. People assume I must love weddings, and that is understandable, since the character I play on my show, *The Mindy Project*, has all but picked the DJ for the fantasy wedding in her head. And as a kid, I actually really loved the idea of having a fancy Judeo-Christian wedding. I remember lying in bed at night when I was eleven and dreaming about walking down the aisle with Dana Carvey, my biggest crush. All his *Saturday Night Live* friends would be on one side of the aisle, and my fifth-grade friends would be on the other. And somehow my parents were fine with me being a child bride, because the Church Lady was so funny and Dana Carvey seemed like a sweet and decent guy. Now that I think about it, if I *had* married Dana Carvey at eleven, that probably would've been a pretty good life.

But the truth is, I really, really don't like weddings.

Here's what I do like: love stories. Romance. In fact, most of my favorite books employ the "marriage plot." What is the "marriage plot," besides the most interesting-sounding movie Katharine Hepburn and Cary Grant never made? This is how I'd explain it. You know how all those movie adaptations of Jane Austen books end with Kate Winslet or Keira Knightley standing outside a chapel in the English countryside in a wedding dress with the man of their dreams? That's the marriage plot. A man and a woman are very attracted to each other but there still seem to be lots of reasons why they can't be together. Sometimes it's logistical (he goes off to war), sometimes it's situational (she's engaged to someone else), sometimes it's emotional (he calls her family tacky and she thinks he's a dickhead). Whatever it is, the audience knows in the back of their heads that these two dum-dums will eventually figure it out and get together and, if we're lucky, there will be a funny sex scene along the way. But that's why I usually love the marriage plot. Because you see everything *except* the wedding.

I find that when I want to take an unpopular opinion about a controversial subject, it's useful to be really organized. The rest of this essay will discuss the various mild injustices that I have experienced at the many weddings I have attended and explain, hopefully compassionately, why I dislike them so much.

There are so few nonreligious rituals we have with our best friends. We can marry our boyfriends and we can baptize our children, but we can't do anything "official" with our best friends, except get matching tattoos of clovers, which no one actually does because who would let a friend do that? So the only real ritual we have is asking each other to be maids of honor or bridesmaids.

Asking your friend to be a bridesmaid is one of the modern paradoxes: no one actually wants to do it, but everyone would be offended if you didn't ask.

And why doesn't anyone want to be a bridesmaid? Because what women who have never done it before don't realize is that, when you are a bridesmaid, you are required to be a literal *maid* for the duration of the wedding. You are in charge of the practicalities and logistics of the ceremony, and not the fun parts, such as providing emotional support, making music playlists, offering fashion advice, and gossiping about which people from college got fat. The only difference between you and an actual maid is that you aren't getting paid and you are supposed to love every second of your job. You even have to wear a uniform: a dress in the same color as the other maids so everyone at the party knows whom to ask when someone is looking for a fridge in which to put her breast milk.

This is particularly outrageous because the groomsmen do absolutely nothing. And I mean *nothing*. Being asked to be a groomsman means you get to give an incredibly inappropriate two-minute speech and every woman there will still want to sleep with you. As a bridesmaid, on the morning of the wedding you will be unfolding the rusty metal legs of a banquet table and in the distance you will see a useless groomsman playing Frisbee with a dog. To rub salt in the wound, he might lightly ask, "Is there anything I can do to help?" knowing full well no self-respecting bridesmaid will task him with any job because he will do it too slowly.

But at least being a bridesmaid is a social activity and can be emotionally rewarding. What is not emotionally rewarding is a honeyfund. There are few things that I have more ideological problems with than the concept of the "honeyfund." Hear me out: I love the idea of giving my newly married friends a meaningful present. But I don't love being asked to be an investor in a crowd-funded honeymoon. Here is why: it's not especially emotionally rewarding to know that I paid for three of five nights of a yurt rental in Big Sur. It's so transactional. Sure, everyone knows all wedding registries are essentially transactional, but at least they are transactional about objects, not about people and experiences. I know you say you have too much stuff in your apartment and what you really want is a killer honeymoon in Thailand. But I feel like, if you have every material good you want, you're probably doing well enough to plan a honeymoon that is within your means. Because a honeymoon is, after all, a sex vacation you're giving yourself after a massive party in your honor.

This brings me to the most common misconception I think couples have about a wedding registry. A gift registry is not about the relationship between man and wife; that's what vows and a marriage are for. The registry is about the relationship between the wedding guest and the couple. It's about your loved ones being able to give you a souvenir of their affection in the form of a tangible house-helpful gift. This is my long-winded way of telling you that you will take my Calphalon wire cooling rack and you will like it.

So why do I participate in any of it? Why not RSVP "no thanks" and hide behind my very busy schedule? Well, a) sometimes I do, and b) when I don't, the simple fact is that the brides are often my closest friends.

With my friends, the sad truth is that our best "best friend" days are behind us. In college, we used to be able to meet each other in the common area of our off-campus housing, excited about our evening ahead, which consisted of someone making an enormous tureen of pasta and drinking wine from a box while we took turns regaling each other with details of our terrible love lives. Playful arguments would become fits of uncontrollable laughter, and, like magic, that experience would be crystallized into a private joke, and the private joke would get boiled down to a simple phrase, which became a souvenir of the entire experience. For years to come, the phrase alone could uncork hours of renewed laughter. And as everyone knows, the best kind of laughter is laughter born of a shared memory.

In my late twenties, when I moved to Los Angeles and all my friends seemed to spread out around the country, I would tell myself, Once I am on hiatus from the show, I will visit them and everything will be the same. But the hiatus would come and go, and a movie role or rewrite job would keep me in L.A. Until I realized: this long expanse of free time to rekindle friendships is not real. We will never come home to each other again and we will never again have each other's undivided attention. That version of our friendship is over forever.

And when I remember this, and it usually happens in those awful, quiet evening hours on Sunday nights, after dinner but before bed, I just lie on my sofa and cry for half an hour. I slip into a melancholy that I know is somehow tied to a deep-seated fear about not being married and having kids myself. Because, at its heart, my annoyance or impatience with my friends' weddings stems from my own panic and abandonment issues. *Why are you leaving me behind like this, friend? What am I supposed to do all by myself now that you are gone?*

It's traumatizing to think that a best friend could become just a friend. That's because there is virtually no difference between an acquaintance and a friend. But the gulf between a friend and a best friend is enormous and profound. And if I look at it that way, I think I can see the value of a wedding. If you're my best friend and the only way I get to have dinner with you is by traveling thousands of miles, selecting a chicken or fish option, and wearing a dress in the same shade of lavender as six other girls, I will do that. I won't love it. But I love you.

MINDY KALING, SORORITY GIRL

THOUGH I WENT TO A VERY ARTSY PRIVATE high school in Cambridge, Massachusetts, I wasn't raised by parents with a liberal attitude toward alcohol. There was no whimsical "sip of wine at Thanksgiving" for us kids while we were still teenagers, like we were in a Noah Baumbach movie. That was for the cool Jewish kids. This was the Clinton era, and my parents were already worried about the moral deterioration of the country. So I drank skim milk with dinner, and did so pretty much every night until I was a story editor at *The Office*.

Thus, I never learned moderation. When I arrived at Dartmouth College in 1997, my attitude toward alcohol was that it was a delicious and dangerous treat that, when obtained, needed to be ingested quickly in case someone tried to take it away. You know, the way a raccoon eats from a garbage can.

People who hear I went to Dartmouth are often surprised by how much I liked it. I think it's because they correctly assume that Dartmouth is extremely white, fairly conservative, outdoorsy, and in the middle of nowhere. And while all these things are true, I still loved it. How is that possible, you ask? How could a nature-hating, sedentary, aspiring (can I still say this?) fag hag feel so at home in rural New Hampshire?

I'll tell you how. All that hunky blond tail is how! Just kidding. I find blond men creepy and unnatural! Just kidding. Every guy hated me! I loved Dartmouth because the minute you set foot on campus, it's like you're in a watercolor painting from your dentist's office called *New England College.* Because it looked so much like the idealized film version of college, I always felt that cinematic college-y things were going to happen to me. Also, most of my fellow students did not look like me or share my interests, which actually made me feel special. Dear old Dartmouth, whose motto is *"Vox Clamantis in Deserto,"* which translated from Latin means "White men crawling out of the forest." In Hanover, New Hampshire, a chirpy, Indian improv comedian who was constantly talking was something of a novelty to the scores of wordless men named Brian. And because Dartmouth was founded in 1769, it had lots of those quintessentially old East Coast college traditions like secret societies, ghost stories, catchy old fight songs that are later deemed racist, and, most important, a Greek system.

For a moment let's pretend that I was born a white man. Chris Christie? *How dare you.* Obviously I would be Jon Lovitz. Now imagine the white male version of me as a freshman at Dartmouth in the late '90s. Kind of a sweet bozo, right? Awful cargo pants, boat shoes, inviting everyone back to the basement of his frat to drink and play pong. This sweet young Lovitz version of me would probably have died of alcohol poisoning before sophomore year, since frat guys had ready, daily access to alcohol and, because at eighteen, I must admit, I loved to drink. At Dartmouth in 1997 you would walk into the basement of any fraternity and there was a 100 percent chance you would find a warm keg of

Bud and a glassy-eyed young man with undiagnosed depression eager to pour you some. I could not have handled that.

Luckily, I was not born a white man.* I was born a socially anxious Indian woman. And while I loved my college and my extracurricular activities, I didn't have access to any kind of parties. Which is why I wanted to be in a sorority.

SEEKING FRIENDSHIPS AS SEEN ON TV

I have a complicated relationship with the Greek system. One side of my personality is absolutely suited for sorority life. I'm an organized person who loves the structure of weekly meetings and scheduled socializing, and I even see the value in hierarchies. I think gentle hazing of the "pledges must wear such-and-such outfits" variety is charming and fun. I am a firm believer that the best friendships come from mandatory time doing tedious chores. Like when a bad kid and a good kid have to spend Saturday cleaning the teachers' lounge and learn they're not so different after all. That said, I do think that perpetrators of some of the worst, most sexist, and most dangerous behavior at Dartmouth were from the Greek system. But, I thought, those are fraternities, not sororities. I'll never make another woman drink her own urine while my friends chant, "Chug! Chug! Chug!" Sure, it's hilarious and probably cements friendships for a lifetime (not to mention I once half-read an article about Madonna drinking her pee for health reasons), but it's wrong. So, I thought, maybe I'll join a sorority.

At Dartmouth, there are many sororities, each with its own reputation. To paint a picture of my options at the time, I will describe some of them now. Please know that these are all subjective, prob-

....
* This has never before been said in the history of humanity.

ably offensive, doubtlessly incorrect sentiments based on attending Dartmouth College in a pre-9/11 era.

Kappa Kappa Gamma—Svelte blond or East Asian women, frequently seen running a seven-minute mile on the treadmills in the Zimmerman Fitness Center, mouthing words to Dixie Chicks songs. Who I would cast in a movie about them: Rosamund Pike.

Delta Delta Delta—Never not smiling, never not baking cookies. Their finely toned arms replace a finely honed sense of irony. Who I would cast in a movie about them: Carrie Underwood.

Kappa Delta Epsilon—Brunette Kappa. Most rumored access to cocaine. Highest proportion of tramp stamps. Sexy party girls who could do cool things like rip a condom open with their teeth. Who I would cast in a movie about them: Mila Kunis.

Sigma Delta—Brassy girls, athletes, drinkers who could "party like the guys." Girls who owned dogs. Feminist and lesbian-friendly. Who I would cast in a movie about them: the background actresses of *Orange Is the New Black*.

Sigma Delt didn't expressly advertise to be the place where minority women interested in the performing arts would thrive, but you know how all the guys who were into theater tech from your high school were also into *Monty Python*? Something about these rowdy rugby-playing lesbians seemed like they would be into my little sketch-comedy plays.

I learned about Sigma Delt because I was a member of a student group called Hanover Crew. Hanover Crew was a group of sophomores, juniors, and seniors selected to welcome incoming freshmen through songs and sketches before they departed for a weeklong outdoor adventure. I applied because it was very exclusive, and I longed for the power trip and free T-shirt that came with it. This school-wide freshman tradition, imaginatively called "Trips," was one of the best experiences I ever had at Dartmouth.

Groups of nervous eighteen-year-olds arrived for their freshman year and were greeted by Hanover Crew. They were then clumped with other freshmen they didn't know to kayak, canoe, hike, and horseback ride through the beautiful White Mountains for a week, and then they all regrouped at the top of Moosilauke Mountain for a night of delicious food, a student-written musical performance, and ghost stories.

Trips lasted three weeks, during which Hanover Crew lived, ate, and slept in the same place, so the fourteen of us grew very close. There were seven guys and seven girls. I was the only sophomore girl and was taken under the wing of two impressive junior girls named Risa and Jeanette. Risa and Jeanette were also in Sigma Delt. Risa was captain of the crew team and the first openly gay woman I had ever met. She looked like Jennifer Garner, had a voice lower than any woman or man on Hanover Crew, and, even now, I have never seen a woman with a body as good as hers. Jeanette was a tiny, stylish, potty-mouthed party girl who wore a blue clip-in extension in her jet-black hair. She taught me how to fill in my eyebrows with an eyebrow pencil. Her catchphrase for whenever anyone was excited or into anything was "Oh my God, they are going to *come their pants.*" To this day, I use this disgusting phrase at least once daily, because I think it must be as incredibly charming as I thought it was in 1998.

I had never met two cooler, more self-actualized, strong women. I followed them around, smitten, and in return Risa and Jeanette adored me. They thought I was funny and subversive because I did things like greet freshmen by saying, "Welcome to Dartmouth College. I am the ghost of a kid who died on her freshman outdoor trip." (I should remind you that there are only, like, twelve funny people in the state of New Hampshire at any given time, so this was pretty impressive.)

By the end of Hanover Crew, after spending all of my time with

Risa and Jeanette, I became infatuated with the idea of being in their sorority. I could hang out with the two coolest upperclassmen I knew and be invited to all their cool activities? They were planning a spaghetti dinner where everyone would watch the Nagano Olympics on their giant flat-screen TV. I remember this detail very clearly. The fact that I had no place to watch the Olympics was stressing me out for some reason.

Pledge season started and, with Jeanette's and Risa's recommendations, I was offered a bid. That moment I will remember forever. The feeling of being offered entry into something old and exclusive was like a drug rush to my young, elitist brain. I accepted, proud of my achievement, ignored the fact that I had done virtually nothing to earn it, and started the pledge process.

PLEASE LIKE ME

I'm going to gently assume that if you're reading this book, you are a little bit of a nerd, or perhaps you're a man whose nerd girlfriend is taking a long time in the bathroom and you can't figure out how to turn on her television, so I need to give you a quick primer on sorority language. "Rush" is the mutual selection period where two things happen: 1) prospective fraternity and sorority members investigate houses and 2) the sororities and frats evaluate the would-be members to see if they'd be a good fit (a.k.a., if they are hot enough to attract members of the opposite sex to their house for parties). After a few weeks of strange little tea parties and "chill barbecues," the frats and sororities ostensibly know enough to offer "bids." Ah, bid day. The day on Dartmouth campus you could see girls either shrieking with happiness in Food Court or, for the unlucky ones, weeping on the phones to their moms, wondering if they should transfer to Duke. Once the bids are accepted, the prospective members become "pledges" and the pledge period begins, lasting for several months until Initiation Night. Initiation Night is usually the most important night of the year for the Greek system, and where most traditions are shared with the youngsters. It can be emotional and moving, or mired in vomit and blood. Sometimes both!

Pledges populated the Dartmouth campus scenery like pine trees, red Solo cups, and built-in-bra tank tops. They were always in some amusing state of mandatory fraternity garb. You could tell a pledge was a Chi Gam because they all wore signs with their names around their necks. Alpha Chi made their pledges grow out facial hair or wear the same plaid shirt for four weeks. Because Dartmouth is in the middle of nowhere, I think giving people secret rituals was also a way of entertaining everyone on campus. I'm the kind of person who encourages her employees to dress up for every holiday—even bank holidays—in a literal-minded way (for example, green and brown for Arbor Day! Leaf earrings!), so I found this gentle sartorial hazing charming.

As a pledge, I was game for all of this. What would Sigma Delt dream up? Pigtails and face paint? Color-coordinated kilts? All any girl wants to do in college is dress like a hot slut and be able to say that it was "mandatory." But they didn't do any of that. All the sisters of Sigma Delt required was for us to show up at events with the other pledges and drink.

I met the other pledges. There was Jenna, the younger cousin of the icy and startlingly thin Sigma Delt recruitment chair, Caitlin (this is not her real name). Caitlin looked like the actress Angie Harmon crossed with a Mexican Day of the Dead skeleton. The cheekbones on Caitlin's stone face could open a bottle of Stoneface. Her gorgeous/alarming appearance was perfect for a powerful senior, because whenever she entered a room your inclination was to stare at her anyway. We all thought her cousin Jenna was incredibly cool and connected. She was in the same extended family as Caitlin! She was there, ostensibly, when the cheekbones first emerged! We were impressed. The only other girl I remember was a small blonde named Maddy, whose main distinguishing trait was that she had been a child actor in *Home Alone 2*, which was something we actually thought was pretty cool. I'm sorry, do *you* have any Macaulay Culkin stories? I don't!

We spent a lot of time together. One afternoon a group of us hiked down to the Connecticut River to cheer on a junior named Abby who had a crew race against Columbia. I did not know Abby, but I went along, face painted with a big green "GO" on my fore-head and "ABBY!" across my cheeks. While we waited, we chatted, and I felt my heart race with the hope and excitement of a good conversation. Did they like comedy? Did they have funny opin-ions about stuff? Jenna steered the conversation with stories of her and Caitlin's family's jointly owned vacation property in the Berk-shires. I actually like hearing about rich people's vacation homes, but only if they're filled with scandalous stuff, like the Kennedy Compound. As Jenna talked about her amazing cousins and the splendor and tranquility of her family's second home, we watched two boats glide by in the distance. Abby was on one of them. If you've never watched a crew race, this is how it goes down: once the boats appear, you scream loudly for nine seconds until they disappear out of view. Then you wait forty minutes for someone to bike over from the finish line and tell you the outcome. It's a little anticlimactic.

That night when I got home, I had a slightly uneasy feeling. I had hugged all the other pledges when we left, and we declared it a "super-fun afternoon," but was it really? It secretly felt more like when someone gives you a holiday card that says "A donation has been made in your honor to such-and-such charity" and all you really wanted was one of those enormous tins of tri-flavored popcorn.

The wonderful thing about being at Sigma Delt was that I was the only person even approximating funny, and therefore I was deemed insanely hilarious. It's a nice feeling when, during a particularly uneventful house meeting, you mime "slitting your wrists out of boredom" and people around you think you are the next Jim Carrey.

Being funny made me well liked, but it also made me the sorority jester. After a night of drinking beer and playing pong, we could go to the basement library, where I was encouraged to do impromptu comedy routines in the center of a circle of sisters. They loved when I would do impressions of guys whom Sigma Delt sisters had slept with, so that was an area I drew from. "Do Andy Trevello!" someone would shout, and I would do my best impression of lacrosse player Andy Trevello, whose defining characteristics were that he was not very smart and rumor had it that he could suck his own penis. You know, just really highbrow, intelligent comedy.

"She is so funny you will *come your pants*," Jeanette said of me on our first pledge night. Now I started to wonder, sadly, If I'm so busy making people come their pants, who is going to make me come mine?*

I looked forward to our Initiation Night, when at last I would break the chains of pledgedom and become a regular sister. We had heard rumors of Initiation Night from Jenna, and how special and sacred it was. I was so excited that I remember calling my mom and saying earnestly, "I think this might be one of the truly memorable nights of my life. I hope I never forget it." She laughed, told me I was over my meal plan by more than $1,000, and asked how many meals I was eating a day. I hung up, a little miffed.

On Initiation Night, we arrived to an empty house full of lit can-

....

* This sentence has also never before been said in the history of humanity.

dles. Ooh, I love this, I thought. This is so very *The Skulls* (starring Paul Walker and Joshua Jackson at the height of their hotness). We were then told to strip down to our bras and underwear (a little gay?, but nice), were blindfolded (gay), made to drink "mysterious libations" (fruit punch laced with vodka), dip our hands in "eerie concoctions" (spaghetti and grapes), and then led downstairs, where the blindfolds were removed and we were standing in the basement surrounded by all of our sisters and twenty pizzas. These were essentially the activities of a kids' Halloween party that a pedophile might throw, but these were the ancient Sigma Delt pledge rituals. It wasn't exactly the secret rituals of the Masons, but it was some enjoyable bonding on a junior varsity level. And what percentage of blindfolded activities end in pizza?

The following week, I missed a Sigma Delt pumpkin-carving party because I had a Latin exam I needed to study for. The next day I received an email from Caitlin about it: "We were just really bummed because we were so excited to see what funny thing you would carve into your pumpkin!" It was sad thinking of hot Día-de-los-Muertos-skeleton Caitlin waiting for me hopefully with a pumpkin. After I missed a Sigma Delt rugby game to go to my Dog Day Players rehearsal, Risa sat me down at the Dirt Cowboy, a cool Seattle-style coffee shop in the middle of town, where people went for serious talks. When she explained what the meeting was about, I was surprised and a little alarmed how closely my attendance was being monitored.

I explained how important my improv troupe was to me, and Risa nodded, serious-faced, with the resolute empathy of someone who has no idea what you are talking about. She leaned in and took my hand. "We're just worried that you're withdrawing from the other sisters. And that maybe you're depressed?"

So much of college is girls labeling other girls terrible things when they don't like their behavior, but using concerned language so they have plausible deniability if they get accused of being bitches: *That girl is not cheerfully doing what the rest of us are doing, so she is probably "depressed" or "has an eating disorder" or "is weird with guys,"* and so on. I was also slowly discovering that I had nothing in common with any of these girls except that we were all excited to see the Nagano Olympics on a big TV.

Even the majesty of the Olympics could not keep me loyal to this group for much longer.

The last straw was one weekend when I was away at Middlebury College with my improv troupe and Sigma Delt was throwing a party with Phi Kap, the fraternity across the street. I couldn't attend, but I wasn't upset because Phi Kap was mostly handsome closeted guys on the diving team, and a chubby Indian freshman girl into improv comedy was probably not a convincing beard. Even your mom would know the jig was up. I mean, why not just come out at that point? So I gladly sat that one out and went to Vermont to do improv. The next afternoon, however, when I arrived back in Hanover, I found a letter had been slid under the door of my dorm room. I was being fined $100 for not reporting to Sigma Delt at eight a.m. to clean up after the party, which was a chore for pledges.

I was outraged. A hundred dollars? To clean up after a party I hadn't even gone to? In my mind, when the good kid and bad kid have to clean up together, it was for camaraderie building. They don't do it because they're going to get *invoiced* if they didn't. I wrote to Jeanette and Risa immediately and told them that Sigma Delt was not for me.

"What??? NOOOOOOOOOO!!! BOOOOOO," wrote Risa. If Jeanette was hurt, she hid it in a very formal tone. "Well, something this serious should not be done over email. You owe it to the sisterhood to meet in person for coffee to discuss this."

You know how girls are always saying that guys broke up with them and it wasn't the breakup itself, it was *the way they did it* that was so uncool? It was around the holidays. It was the week of her mother's birthday. It was on the phone. And you are listening, thinking, *So, the only decent way for him to have broken up with you is to not break up with you and stay with you forever?*

That is what Sigma Delt was doing to me. I finally understood how guys felt.

So I met Jeanette and Risa at the Dirt Cowboy to break up the right way. Before I could say anything, Jeanette coldly asked if I was an only child. I said no. "I'm very surprised," she said. As an education major, she said I displayed qualities that an only child would have. Risa was less angry, and was just sad. "It's just . . . you're so funny. The impressions. The song parodies. Who will make us come our pants?"

There was a long silence during which I suspect I was expected to cry. I couldn't muster up tears, but I did do some low moaning, like this decision was causing me physical pain. "Ohhhh, this sucks," I moaned. "It's so unfair!" I said, as though the choice to leave was somehow being forced upon me, a trick boys would later employ on me to extricate themselves from dating me. Karma, I guess. Finally, though, I couldn't beat around the bush anymore, and guiltily asked: "Can I please sign the paper to deactivate?" I signed it, they left, I finished my hot chocolate, and I never set foot in Sigma Delt again.

I thought I would like an environment of all women, where I was deemed the "funny one." But it took me twelve weeks to realize that I don't really like organizations where people are "deemed" things. I should mention that I did learn a few undeniably useful things at my sorority, like: a) the trick to getting any guy to fall in love with you is to laugh at everything he says and touch your mouth a lot, and b) in a pinch, you can wash your bras in a salad spinner. The problem with joining a sorority was that I was a person who wanted to make friends based on common interests. And our common interests had to be more than simply wanting to make friends. As someone who enjoys secrets, exclusivity, and elitism (I basically live to one day meet someone who owns an American Express Black Card), I was surprised and sad when I realized I was never meant to be Greek.

Ultimately, I got out of the Greek system unscathed. Later I would read accounts of pledging at Dartmouth where it seemed like everyone was given alcohol poisoning and then ordered to set fire to the music library in the nude or something. I did not have that experience, and I know many friends who loved their sororities. I wasn't traumatized. I was just bored.

(MINOR) FAME HAS CHANGED ME

WHEN I WAS ON *THE OFFICE*, I WAS THE perfect kind of famous: a little bit famous. Double-take-at-the-airport famous. Occasionally someone would come up to me and excitedly say, "That's what she said!" and I would smile knowingly and respond, "Steve's great, isn't he?" implying that Steve Carell and I are very close friends who vacation together.

Now things are a little different. To clarify: I'm by no means *famous*-famous, like Rihanna or a Kardashian or Nicki Minaj's butt. Those are people who have to wear makeup when they exercise, which is a whole other tier of fame.

Being known is really fun, extremely strange, and not very important. This is what it's like.

THESE ARE THE THINGS I CAN NO LONGER DO NOW THAT I'M FAMOUS

Bargain for Stuff

Like every normal person, when I go to a flea market, I don't want to be the chump who pays the asking price for anything. But recently, my friend B. J. Novak pointed out that loudly bargaining in public is unbecoming for actresses with their own TV shows. His theory is that people think I'm filthy rich and no one wants to see that either a) I'm not rich, and how alarming is that, because what kind of drug problem could I have where I frittered away all my TV-show money and now have to bargain at the flea market?! or b) I'm rich and cheap, which is universally regarded as the worst thing you can be.

Say Offensive Things

Look, would I love to be able to freely spout the gently racist/sexist stuff that sometimes crosses my mind when I'm the worst version of myself? Sure! That's part of my candid, first-generation-immigrant charm! One Saturday afternoon several summers ago, I went to visit my friend Brenda in Provincetown, Massachusetts. Provincetown has a large gay population, and during the summer there are even more gay tourists. Brenda and I were trying to walk down their main street, and we were slowed down by throngs of gay tourists walking very slowly, taking in the sights and sounds. Frustrated, I wanted to say, *Man, this place is gay as hell!* but I didn't. I didn't want people to go home and tell their friends that that girl from *The Mindy Project* found something "too gay." I would never want a homophobic reputation, for many reasons, the most important being that I am aspiring to be a tragic gay cult icon. Also, it is wrong. So I just let out a frustrated sound and said, "Crowds!" I actually think this new self-awareness has made me a better person.

Online Dating

Sadly, I believe the legitimization of online dating coincided with my becoming a little bit famous. Even in the mid-2000s, my friends online dated but acknowledged that they felt like slightly desperate creeps doing it. Now even my coolest friends are online dating. But not me. I live in fear of my public profile being published online for everyone to see. Especially since I am such a liar. On a dating profile page, I would pretend to be a completely different person. You would see me loving live music and hiking. You basically leave the date thinking I'm an outdoorsy Stevie Nicks.

Frown

About a year ago, I had lunch with Reese Witherspoon in Brentwood* to discuss a project we were thinking of working on, and when we walked out to our cars, a couple of photographers were waiting to take her photo. She whispered to me, "Smile." "Why?" I asked. "We're just walking to our cars." Reese responded "No one who sees a photograph of us wants to see that we are anything other than totally happy all the time." At first I thought that couldn't possibly be true, but then, on the drive home, I realized how correct Reese was. When I see a photo in *US Weekly* of Angelina Jolie-Pitt walking back to her car from the pharmacy, I feel a little irrationally miffed if she's not smiling. She has a great life and, like, twenty gorgeous kids! Why are you not smiling, Angelina Jolie-Pitt?! If you're not grinning ear-to-ear when you're sleeping with Brad Pitt every night, then how shitty is *my* life?

So now I get it, and I have tried to train my face to be a smile in repose instead of the low-level grimace I've worn my whole life. Also, I comb my bangs over my acne and wear aviator sunglasses like Tom Cruise so people will really be psyched when they see an impromptu paparazzi photo of me. Stars are just like us (but they are super happy and grateful every moment, even when they are picking up UTI medicine)!

....
* Jealous, haters?

Complain

This is related to frowning. Nobody wants to hear that any aspect of my awesome life is bad. I get that.

But there are days, maybe two or three times a year, when I get completely overwhelmed by my job and go to my office, lie on the floor, and cry for ten minutes. Then I think: *Mindy, you have literally the best life in the world besides that hot lawyer who married George Clooney. This is what you dreamed about when you were a weird, determined little ten-year-old. There are more than a thousand people in one square mile of this studio who would kill to have this job. Get your ass up off the floor and go back into that writers' room, you weakling.* Then I get up, pour myself a generous glass of whiskey and club soda, think about the sustained grit of my parents, and go back to work.

I know that made me sound like a tortured alcoholic, like Don Draper, but I swear I'm not.

OK, I'm done complaining, because *of course* there's lots of cool stuff I get to do now that I'm famous.

THINGS I *CAN* DO NOW THAT I'M
A LITTLE BIT FAMOUS

Contact Jai Courtney If I Need To

Listen, it's not like I have handsome Australian action star Jai Courtney's phone number on speed dial or anything, but if there was a life-or-death emergency, or, more reasonably, if I was dying and my dying wish was to have "Make-a-Wish"–style sex with Jai Courtney, I bet I could swing that. My friend Ike knows him.

People Sometimes Send Me Stuff

For my birthday last year, McDonald's sent me a sweet stack of $10 gift cards. If you follow me on any kind of social media you will see that I'm constantly eating McDonald's, and not in a campy, skinny-actress way where I go when I'm on my period and "being bad!" I go regularly enough that the woman at the Crescent Heights & Sunset McDonald's gives me ranch and buffalo sauce packets for my McNuggets without me having to ask. I think McDonald's was hoping I would share my gift cards with my cast and writers, but I don't.

Guys in Prison Email Me

Ever heard of Corrlinks.com? No? Neither had I! Probably because Corrlinks is the official email system used by the federal penitentiary system. It's for inmates who want to communicate with the outside world. About two years ago, a month after *The Mindy Project* premiered, my inbox was flooded with emails from this mysterious site called "Corrlinks," requesting that I accept their invitations for communication. At first my mind went to "cuff links" and I thought it was some fashion-related website. Nope.

I guess *The Mindy Project* was popular in certain federal prisons and because of that, coupled with the fact that my email address was incredibly easy to guess (I have since changed it!), I was getting a lot of requests. At first I was kind of flattered and amused; I liked thinking of all the guys in the prison rec room quieting down when the show came on. "Shut up, you guys!" one inmate would menacingly shout to another one, who is playing Ping-Pong. "I hope Mindy manages to find a good balance between work and dating!" "Danny is soulful and closed off, just like my cellmate!" "Where's the old doctor?" "Why do they keep changing the cast?" "The warden isn't looking, let's riot!"

But then, just as I was beginning to enjoy it, it became a little scary. I would return from set and there would be more and more emails requesting to initiate contact with me. Guys with names like "Robert Lee" and "Rufus." I imagine the flipside of an unrequited prison crush is prison rage. I also don't live in any kind of gated community, and my house is very easy to break into. I've broken into it twice when I couldn't find my keys, and I'm not even a hardened criminal (yet)! So, with a heavy heart, I went through the process of blocking requests from Corrlinks.

I do like the distinction that these were federal prisoners trying to contact me, not state prisoners. Federal prisons are way more fancy, so, in my mind, these were fairly classy guys. Large-scale drug traffickers and *Wolf of Wall Street*–type guys rather than stab-and-grabbers. I mean, no offense to stab-and-grabbers, especially hot ones.

Be Compared to Other Famous Women

One rite of passage I experienced is that I am now known enough to be featured on a magazine's "Who Wore It Best?" page. "Who Wore It Best?" is incredibly popular because we, as consumers, are not completely satisfied with our scrutiny of women's appearances in TV and film. We also find it enjoyable to pit women against each other in fashion Hunger Games.

To determine who wore it best, a group of strangers is polled on the street on their way to lunch somewhere in midtown Manhattan (if I have learned anything from watching TV, it's that stopping people on a busy Manhattan street is the fairest and most democratic way to get the true answer to something).

"Who wore this Stella McCartney dress better?" a tired magazine intern asks, presenting two photos of actresses wearing the same dress and secretly wondering if taking a semester off from college to work at this publication was the best use of her time. "Was it comedy TV actor Mindy Kaling? Or was it internationally famous supermodel Gisele Bündchen?"

After hours of asking people this question, the results are in! Ninety-nine percent think Gisele wore it better. One percent say

Mindy wore it better, and that was a blind woman who was looking for a bathroom.

I can actually save the magazine editors behind "Who Wore It Best?" some time. Here's the answer 100 percent of the time: it's always the more famous or classically beautiful woman!

I laugh thinking about if they ever tried to do "Who Wore It Best?" for men's magazines. They wouldn't, because no one would care. Men don't care which men looked better in the same clothes because it's so obviously a huge waste of time. It's also why they don't have astrology sections in men's magazines.

Cool Women Want to Be My Best Friend

One very gratifying compliment I sometimes hear is that women want to be my best friend. This endlessly amuses my actual best friend, Jocelyn, because in her estimation I'm "a good friend, but not *that* great." Here are the pros of being best friends with me: I am one of the best people you could take to your ex-boyfriend's birthday party that you were dreading going to. I am always up for dessert. I am always up for skinny-dipping. If you want to talk to any hot guy at any party, I will so be that girl who gets drunk and introduces us, then inches away so you can roll your eyes about me and sell me out so you can bond with him. I will dance almost anywhere with anyone. I have one of the sickest closets of clothes, and I will let you borrow anything and spend hours doing fashion shows in my bedroom with you. There are no cons.

Change People's Lives

The single best outcome of my (minor) fame is that women—usually young women who feel marginalized for some reason—come up to me, or write to me, to tell me I make them feel more "normal." That is profoundly moving to me. I'm not saying I'm some kind of pioneer here, like, Indian Dorothy Dandridge or whoever, but I love that. I'm a role model now. It makes all the stuff I can't do anymore completely worth it. It's actually the way that my (minor) fame has changed me the most. I want to be a better person because I don't want to disappoint those girls. I stop and think about my actions more. I tip great, I try not to swear too much, and I remember to thank people and be grateful. And all that stuff I do to "appear" better has actually made me a better person. I wish I had always acted like I was a little bit famous.

THINGS TO BRING TO MY DINNER PARTY

I F I HOST A DINNER PARTY AT MY HOUSE that you are invited to, then first of all: congratulations! You are living in a thrilling science-fiction world where robots probably walk among humans as equals, and also, I know how to cook.

I spent a great deal of my youth fantasizing about entertaining. In my early twenties I would spend hours poring over cookbooks at the Seventh Avenue Barnes & Noble in Park Slope, planning elaborate parties that I would throw when I was older and had money. Now I am older and have money, but I almost never entertain. I have yet to throw my *Great Gatsby*–themed Super Bowl viewing party, but when I do, it will be a big hit, as will be my Daisy Buchanan slow-cooker chicken enchiladas.

It is more than ten years later and, in some ways, I am the person I hoped I'd turn out to be when I was twenty-three. I mean, I hoped I would be married to a Laker and have an Oscar and an ass that doesn't quit, but I'm doing pretty well. I do not, however, throw nearly enough dinner parties. But if I ever do, you will *never* be asked to bring anything. I believe the potluck tradition of entertaining is the equivalent of a teenage boy wanting to have sex with his girlfriend but who is too scared to go to CVS to buy condoms. If you can't handle providing all the courses for your dinner party, you can't handle the hosting duties of a dinner party.

However, if you *feel like* bringing the following non-food items, boy, will you be my favorite guest. Here's what I suggest you bring:

A great story about a near-death experience. Did you ever get mugged at gunpoint on the subway late at night? Did you ever almost fall over the ledge of the Grand Canyon Skywalk? Did you ever have dinner at a restaurant the same night a serial murderer also ate there? Are you a ghost? Tell that story, please!

A great story about a scandalous celebrity experience. Did you ever hook up with Jimmy Fallon before he was famous? And was he into something in bed that would surprise and titillate us? Oh my! Please go on!

My mail from my mailbox. Thanks, bud. Just leave it on the counter. You're a good friend.

An old picture of us you found.

We looked like that in college? Ahhh, we were so weird!

An old picture of Colin Firth you found.

Oh là là. No need for dessert, am I right? (Don't worry, there's obviously also dessert.)

A new kind of hot sauce you want to introduce me to. I eat hot sauce on approximately 70 percent of my meals. Learning about new hot sauces is the least expensive way to improve my quality of life. Remember when I tried Sambal Oelek and I wouldn't shut up about it? This is a very thoughtful gift that shows a deep understanding of your hostess.

Your ukulele to play a song after dinner. Classic tunes only, like "Over the Rainbow," or songs that would sound funny on the uke, like Sam Smith's "Stay with Me." No original music allowed! You know I can't stand original music! Please stick to the hits. This is a celebratory event, not an open mike night at the Campus Events Hall.

An enormous vintage diamond engagement ring you are giving to me because you are going to announce at dinner that I am yours. I can't believe it! I'm being proposed to at my own fussy dinner party even though I had all these irritating restrictions! I'm the luckiest girl on earth!

A huge appetite and a cheerful tolerance for solid B-minus cooking. Just a friendly reminder: I truly cannot cook.

PLAYER

WAS AT A FRIEND'S BIRTHDAY PARTY AT ONE of those bars in downtown L.A. where the cocktail waitresses have to dress up like Sally Bowles and take your drink orders in character. I was twenty-five and pretending to like the taste of absinthe. I had just been dumped by Nate, a guy I'd dated briefly. Nate was a comedy writer I had met at the gym. Every week or so he would wander over while I was on the elliptical machine and make small talk. Well, small talk for a comedy writer, which meant asking me nervously about some perceived environmental hazard at our gym. Once he asked if I thought there was asbestos coming out of the air-conditioner duct. Another time if the towels smelled like mildew. Every time, I told him no. I never think environmental hazards are going to kill me. I only think serial killers are.

After months of thinking he was simply a friendly hypochondriac whose neuroses extended to bothering strangers while they did cardio, Nate asked me out. He turned out to be cooler than I thought, and I was impressed by his opinions about movies and music: he liked nothing unless he knew someone personally involved (I was twenty-five, this was a cool attitude to have then).

But after two months of dating, he stopped calling me. Perhaps it was because I was never as alarmed about our health safety as he was; maybe it was because it was clear I wasn't going to have sex for months and months (again, I was twenty-five); maybe he just thought I was lame. I will never know. It surprisingly hurt my feelings, because I made the mistake of talking about him excitedly to my friends, and then it was over.

So it was not a great night at this Sally Bowles bar. It was a birthday party for a friend of a friend, but the first friend ended up not being able to go, so I was stuck with a room full of strangers. I could've bailed, but I was feeling a little lonely and therefore susceptible to a naïve spurt of positivity where I convinced myself: *Who cares if you don't know anyone? That's the only way to* meet *someone!*

Of course, Nate was there, and he was making animated chit-chat across the bar with a briefcase model from *Deal or No Deal*. She didn't have her briefcase with her or anything, but people kept marveling about it. Something about having the prop of a briefcase made this model go from simply "hot" to "hot and interesting." It was like the briefcases were fooling people into thinking all these models were not human display cases but in fact accomplished businesswomen. I was wearing a black pinafore-style dress with a long-sleeved T-shirt underneath, which, when I was getting dressed at home, seemed very stylish and French. But suddenly, in the face of the unabashed hotness of a *Deal or No Deal* girl, I felt like a middle-aged au pair for a family in the Pacific Palisades. I was nursing an absinthe because, though I loathe any alcoholic drink that isn't brimming with maraschino cherries, this was the specialty drink of the venue, and I was in the kind of mood where I desperately wanted to fit in.

After fifteen minutes of trying to make friendly eye contact with people and failing, I sighed and decided it was time to go home, figuring that if I left now I could pick up a Filet-O-Fish from the McDonald's drive-thru and still catch "Weekend Update" on *SNL*. The number of times I have bailed on something on a Saturday night with the hopes that I could be "home in time for 'Weekend Update'" is in the dozens. Somehow if I made it back in time to see Amy Poehler and Tina Fey's take on the news, the night would not have been a total bust.

I was pulling cash out of my clutch to pay when I saw her.

IT IS THE EAST AND GRETA IS THE SUN

Entering the speakeasy was a beautiful pale girl with long shiny blond hair, dressed in torn jeans and Converse, a plaid shirt tied sloppily around her shoulders. She was the only girl in the bar not wearing heels, and definitely the only person at the bar besides the busboys wearing sneakers. She carried an enormous Chanel bag. She was at once underdressed and overqualified for this party, and was instantly the coolest person there. She made eye contact with me, smiled, waved, and headed toward me. I smiled back. I did not know her.

Had we gone to high school together? Was she that friendly nameless girl who got me a glass of water when I had my hair cut? I blotted my shiny cheeks and nose, suddenly sweating like I do when I meet a guy I like. Am I gay?, I thought, wondering why I was so nervous. When she finally made her way to me at the bar, she stopped and covered her mouth with her hands in a look of utter delighted shock. "I'm sorry," she said. "Can I just hug you, please? We don't know each other, but I'm obsessed with you." Puzzled but incredibly flattered, I nodded. She then gave me the warmest and sweetest-smelling hug I have ever received. "My name is Greta," she said. "And we are going to be best friends."

Two things you should know are that Greta is not her real name and I am not a hugger. For the record, in New York, that is a perfectly acceptable way to be. If you hug someone there they are either a person in your immediate family whom you have not seen in months, or they are gravely ill. In Los Angeles, however, if you're not hugging everyone hello and goodbye you are considered to be a total asshole with anger problems. But Greta's embrace was so full of love, and I was so sad and insecure, that it was like being wrapped in the coziest blanket.

Greta became my date for the evening and was the wing-woman I had always wanted. She was pretty enough to be an actress but thought the idea was absurd. She was, from what I could tell, some kind of freelance creative producer/consultant/tastemaker. Someone whispered to me that she was fourth-generation Yale but had dropped out to work for MTV in Hong Kong. She knew everyone at the party and, from what I could see, everyone was delighted to see her. And though this was the first time I had ever met her, she was giving me career advice with the kind of confidence that made me feel like it was 100 percent correct. Greta introduced me to people and then pulled me aside after. "You *must* get coffee with Stacy. She's stylish, she gets it, *she's someone you should know.*" I nodded, taking this very seriously. *She's someone you should know.* I had never heard this phrase and now it was the most important phrase of my life.

About Nate and the *Deal or No Deal* girl, Greta rolled her eyes and assured me: "You have nothing to worry about. She's just a Tiffany in American Apparel leggings. You've outgrown Nate, anyway." "Her name is Tiffany?" I asked. Greta wrinkled her nose. "No. Tiffany is her essence." She did not know Nate, and she did not know me, but I believed her, because I liked the idealized version of me that she saw, even though we were strangers. Whatever Greta saw? That's what I wanted to be. We spent the evening at the bar laughing and drinking, and we exchanged phone numbers. She texted me on the way home.

GRETA: Nate can (_X_)
ME: ???
GRETA: Kiss my butt!

I felt a tugging in my chest and recognized it as love.

AT LONG LAST, MY LONG-LOST LOVE

The week after I met Greta, I started the hiatus between seasons 1 and 2 of *The Office*, which is like our summer vacation. Greta was suddenly with me everywhere. She was always available to hang out, and when we did she was a blast. It is not hard to have fun with someone who thinks you are the funniest and most fabulous celebrity she has ever met. But she wasn't just some random sycophant. Greta told me when I wore an outfit that was unflattering, which was how I knew she was real. And she would do it the best way anyone had ever given me an insult: "You have so much more to offer than that skirt. Find a skirt that deserves you." But her candor did not make her edgy or cynical. Quite the opposite. Greta was so sweet, she was completely intoxicating. She never seemed to dislike or hate *anything*, no movie or TV show, no matter how bad it was. We saw *Poseidon* and as we walked out of the theater she said, "It must have been challenging to do a movie with so much water." And her positivity had a great effect on me. I was no longer the frowning comedy writer with my arms crossed in skepticism. I liked things! It was so nice to have someone in my life who was not caustic or judgmental.

Greta was also a massive resource for all things Los Angeles, having moved there from New York with her family when she was twelve. When I complained of being tired, Greta recommended her "exhaustion guy." She wasn't like my lame parents who said that I needed to sleep more and eat better to combat tiredness. Greta's solution was pharmaceutical and therefore much more fun. She recommended that I get B-complex shots from a guy she knew named Doug. Doug was not exactly a doctor, but he had some kind of degree and kept his prices low by using the storage closet of a Culver City health-food store as his clinic. I was willing to try anything that would make me feel better and required no lifestyle changes, so Doug was a great solution. It also helped that Greta mentioned Doug was the "exhaustion guy" for a handful of energetic and skinny celebrities I admired, one of whom I had seen in my spinning class *destroying*, a mere two weeks after giving birth naturally. If I ever give birth naturally (never going to happen), I will never sit upon a bike again. I'm not very in touch with my body, but I would never do that to my vagina.

The "clinic" was windowless and no bigger than a handicapped bathroom stall. I sat around for fifteen minutes, looking at all the boxes of Latisse and facial injectables available for purchase. Doug appeared, clad in an Affliction waffle-knit tee and True Religion jeans. It was 2006, so this was a sign of great success. Doug was very busy and a little brusque. He said he was only seeing me "because you're friends with Greta." Without asking me any of my medical information he swiped an alcohol wipe over my love handle, gave me a quick jab of B-complex, and told me to come back the next week.

When I tried to pay, he shook his head. "I take care of Greta's people."

It had only been a month, but I was now one of Greta's people. I felt exclusive and Jewish. This was my favorite club.

ARIEL AND AMANDA AND CHIARA AND KELSEY

Greta had an enormous group of girlfriends. They were all viva-cious L.A. girls with lots of style and personality, all involved in offshoots of Hollywood entertainment, with many specific things in common: they were rich, thin, white, and in search of meaning for their lives.

I found myself sitting cross-legged on the floors of living rooms of mansions all over Los Angeles, attending trunk shows and book clubs and self-empowerment classes in homes with catered lun-cheon spreads where no one ate but me. Greta's girlfriends would tell bawdy stories in white jeans and had old, ugly husbands.

I absolutely loved it. I had no friends like this at all, people so quintessentially "L.A." My friends were neurotic brown-haired people from the tristate area or New England.

And their names! Oh, the names. Greta's friends had the best names: Ariel the jewelry designer. Chiara the celebrity makeup artist. Amanda the hand model. Kelsey who ran PR for a clothing brand of slutty sweaters that are very popular. I was in girly name heaven. When you grow up with the name Mindy, it's not the best. In addition to a lifetime of gym teachers trying to create rapport with you by asking "How is Mork doing?" it didn't have the frilly feminin-ity of the names I really coveted. "Mindy" is the name of a bank teller or a babysitter, but not even the hot babysitter who you hope will tell you about French kissing. Mindy is the responsible babysitter who makes you do your homework and go to bed before *Cheers*.

Meanwhile, my real best friend, Jocelyn, who lived in New York, was getting mildly irritated by photos of Greta and me surfacing on Facebook. Jocelyn was my best friend from the first week of college. She and I had lived together all through Dartmouth, and then in New York City for three years before I moved to Los Angeles. She would come to my house for Thanksgiving every year, and I am now the godmother to her son. She's an excellent example of what a hip-hop artist might call a "ride-or-die bitch." And I missed her. I missed female friendship! I had no real girlfriends in the year I moved to Los Angeles from New York. My only pals were my work friends, and they were mostly older married guys who barely understood their phones.

"Who the hell is Greta?" Jocelyn asked one Sunday afternoon on the phone. "Why did she tag you in a photo album called 'BFFs'?!" she demanded. Jocelyn and I had long made fun of terms like "BFF" and "girl crush." To us, they signified the infantilization of women, and we were way too sophisticated for that. We had lived in Brooklyn near Jonathan Safran Foer! But hanging out with Greta had dulled my critical eye, because, frankly, it felt good to be called someone's "BFF." And when had a critical eye ever helped me, really? Nobody likes the girl who points out all the inherent sexism on *The Bachelor*. But people are charmed by the girl kvelling about nail art, boba tea, and the homeopathic benefits of ayahuasca.

THE VACCINATION TRAP

I was at a baby shower with Greta for an extremely famous pop singer. The pop singer had turned her enormous backyard into a miniature World's Fair for children, complete with gluten-free everything and a woman whose job it was to do face-paint designs so intricate they rivaled the work done on *Pirates of the Caribbean*.

However, the children were not having a good time. The reason? One little girl had been jumping on the trampoline, and when she touched the metal frame, which had been sitting in the sun, she screamed "too hot!" and burst into tears. She was subsequently circled by adults examining her "burned" leg, which turned out to be nothing. The damage was done, however. Now none of the children at the party would touch anything for fear of it being "too hot." The party moved inside, where there was nothing to do but drink.

Unfortunately, for me, "nothing to do but drink" tends to mean "nothing to do but get into trouble."

I drink when I don't know a lot of people, which is a useful habit I picked up in college. When I am a bit tipsy, I am instantly cheerful and not so socially anxious. The key is that I can drink no more than two drinks because, after that, I go from making charming small talk to slurred rants.

Three Champagnes in, the pop singer brought up that she was firing her pediatrician and asked if anyone could recommend a doctor. One of my acquaintances from college, Asha, was a pediatrician in Santa Monica, so I excitedly recommended her, thinking this would be the beginning of a lifetime of Asha and me getting free tickets to see the pop star at the Staples Center. Imagine, me and Asha being pulled up onstage to get sung to! Why would *I* be invited, you ask? As the middleman, of course.

POP STAR: Oh, that's so great. I'm really looking for someone young and cool. My last guy had really antiquated ideas.
ME: Asha is the best. And very young and cool. Unless of course you don't want to get your kids vaccinated, hahaha.

The pop star froze and everyone went silent. Greta looked at me, eyes widening in horror. I could not have offended a group of people more quickly than if I had announced to a room of male comedy writers that the movie *Caddyshack* sucks (which I have done, and which did not go over very well). The point is, people were incredibly offended.

POP STAR: (*icily*) I'm actually leaving my pediatrician because of his outdated position on vaccinations and autism.

Now, had I been one Champagne in, I could've backtracked so deftly you would think I was Michael Jackson moonwalking across the stage on his *Bad* world tour. Even two Champagnes and I could've charmed my way out of this by pretending I was being ironic the whole time. But not three. Three glasses of anything alcoholic is like truth serum for me.

MINDY: (*slurry rant*) Oh God, Pop Star! Say it ain't so. Say you aren't one of those crazy Hollywood people who doesn't believe in vaccination.

I glanced at Greta. Greta's gaze was on the ground. Oh, no.

POP STAR: (*stone cold*) Actually, I am.

Within ninety seconds, Greta and I were in her Fiat, headed down Doheny out of the hills. I could see the worry pass over her eyes as we drove home. *What will Mindy say about at-home births? Kabbalah? My psychic?* She was silent and turned up the Justin Timberlake. We didn't even stop for frozen yogurt on the way home. It was the closest to furious I had ever seen her.

The frayed edges of Greta's and my relationship became more apparent. Her sweetness and accommodating personality also extended to beliefs that I ridiculed, and even thought were bad for humanity.

Still, Greta was all about forgiveness and getting over stuff. I had messed up, but she would look past it. She hugged me before

I got out of the car and said she would call. I breathed a sigh of relief.

GONE BABY GONE

At the end of July, work started up again at *The Office*. I was back on the schedule of six-a.m. call times and staying in the writers' room until nine p.m. We still grabbed dinner or got exhaustion shots sometimes, but I couldn't go with Greta to screenings and baby showers anymore. In the beginning, Greta was fine with my busyness. We kept in close touch, texting at least twenty times a day. But then, as the weeks went by, I heard from Greta less and less. She told me she was working more, though for the life of me I still could not pinpoint exactly what her job was. One weekend in September, I was miffed that she couldn't get iced green teas with me. I texted: "I MISS you!" and "Why are we not getting frozen yogurt together right now?!" using all the emoticons Greta herself had taught me. But more and more, my texts went unanswered. Once I read down our text chain and saw she had written the exact phrase "Hey QT. Love you miss you xoxo" three times, like it had been copied and pasted.

In mid-October, on Facebook, I saw photos of Greta after booty ballet class with a gorgeous actress in her early twenties whom I recognized as the former second lead on a Disney Channel show I will call *Dixie Peppard, Secret Singer-Songwriter and Witch*. Greta was tagged and the caption was: "Doing booty ballet with my BFF. Can barely walk!" I clicked on this photo and saw even more photos of Greta and Second Lead. Greta and Second Lead in Malibu. Greta and Second Lead at a Dodgers game. Greta and Second Lead at a Beverly Hills hair salon getting "lobs" (long bobs) together.

I had been replaced by a younger model. And now they had matching long bobs.

The sting of being replaced was very painful. Thank God this was pre-Twitter, because I know I would've tweeted a lot of angry quotes about betrayal and then later deleted them in a worried state. Greta's phasing me out of her life hurt way more than Nate. Hell, it hurt way more than most breakups I'd had, and we were only friends for about four months. But as any woman reading this will attest to, there are not many relationships more powerful than that of two women who fall fast and deep into a friendship. It was heartbreaking to be loved and left.

Happily, though, a few months later, work had taken over my entire life, and my friend group was whittled down to the old reliable standbys: Mom, Jocelyn, Brenda, and B.J. None of them would love the term "old reliable standby," so shhh, don't tell them. The great thing about true best friends is that when you go MIA for a few months, they inquire but they don't press. Best friends know the power of infatuation but also how quickly it dissipates. You just have to wait it out. And then afterward, tease them about it for decades.

In the past ten years, I have met a handful of chic and charismatic women in Los Angeles with whom I have had the telltale spark of being "best-friend material." It's exciting, like seeing a guy you are really attracted to from across the room at a party. None, however, has managed to infiltrate deep into my best-friend group, where they have seen me openly weep, heard me talk shit about my job, or checked my scalp for worrisome alopecia spots. But one magical summer, Greta was my best friend. And then, like the guy who spends the night and the next morning tells you, "I honestly feel like I've never met anyone like you before," she was gone.

Take This Job
and Love It

HOW TO GET YOUR OWN TV SHOW
(AND NEARLY DIE OF ANXIETY)

THOUGH I AM EXTREMELY YOUNG, I AM old enough to remember Must-See TV. For the small handful of readers who are even younger than me and don't know what I'm talking about, Must-See TV refers to the Thursday-night lineup on NBC in the '80s and '90s, when you could watch back-to-back, amazing, high-quality shows like *The Cosby Show*, *Cheers*, *Seinfeld*, and *Friends*. I had the unique experience of being hired to work at NBC in 2004, the year *Friends* ended, which marked the death of that dynasty. Over the next eight years, Must-See TV went from Must-See TV to Pretty Good TV to Not the Worst Thing on TV to Meh, Just Watch HBO TV.

I was lucky enough to be employed at one of the remaining great NBC shows of the mid-2000s, *The Office*. Greg Daniels, the creator of the American version of *The Office*, had plucked me from a strange little off-Broadway play, *Matt and Ben*, which I had cowritten and in which I played Ben Affleck, to write on his show.*

....

* If this is too interesting-sounding to toss off in an essay about something else, please read my essay about it in my first book. I bet your older sister or maybe-secretly-gay best guy friend has it somewhere.

In eight years *The Office* went from near-cancellation to the kind of mainstream and critical success where people come up to you and ask, "Is Dwight really like that in real life?" to which I respond: "Oh, no, Rainn isn't like Dwight. Dwight is an *angel* next to Rainn. Rainn is a demon."

In the fall of 2011, I was feeling pretty good about myself. I had been working on *The Office* for almost eight years. I was thirty-one years old and was one of the few people in TV who felt like I had job stability.

As the success of *The Office* grew, so did my role as a writer and producer, and by season 8 I had written twenty-four episodes. I was invited to be on cool talk shows like *The Tonight Show* and *The Late Show with David Letterman*, and Dave and Paul Shaffer didn't even have to pretend to know the show that I was on.

I got to see my friend B. J. Novak daily, which, when we weren't fighting, was the absolute best. Greg and I were nominated for an Emmy for writing the "Niagara" episode, where Jim and Pam get married. But perhaps best of all, I had enough pull that the writers' assistant kept the fridge stocked with my favorite junk foods—Australian red licorice and Pepperidge Farm cinnamon raisin bread—without my even asking. If that isn't success and power, I don't know what is.

Most TV writers, even the good ones, aren't usually lucky enough to be employed on a great show. And even great shows get canceled. Most writers have to hop from gig to gig to pay for their Priuses and private schools and divorces. I was an exception. I had what most writers dream of: a consistent source of free lunch for eight years. I was a member of the core creative team of what some people considered a classic American comedy, with no end in sight. And did I appreciate it? Um . . . *sometimes?*

The truth was, I had started growing a little restless. I had a dream job—was I ungrateful to wonder what more there might be for me? Or complacent if I didn't? The fights in the writers' room and the outcomes that didn't go my way, the one or two great lines a week on-camera, and, of course, the snacks—was there more to life than an endless supply of Australian red licorice (OK, obviously not, that stuff's amazing, but you know what I mean)?! And who was I to try to seek anything better? In high school I had been cast as a rag-picker/townsperson/vagrant in eight consecutive plays. Why would I think I could be anything more than part of an ensemble of anything? These conflicting feelings about my job were illuminating—I was finally experiencing what they call "White People Problems." Or, maybe because of my socioeconomic background, this is more of a "First World Problem"? Or a "One Percenter" issue? I can't pinpoint which conflict of privilege I was experiencing, but you get it.

THE SOMEWHAT YOUNG AND THE RESTLESS

In television, no matter what your title is, no matter how much you contribute, the only person who has the final say is the show-runner.

When you aren't the showrunner on a TV show, you feel like a highly regarded attorney: you work hard, do the research, and argue your case, but the judge (in this case, Greg, or Paul Lieberstein, who played Toby on the show and became showrunner after Greg) gets to decide what will actually happen.

And though you understand the pecking order and respect the judge—and even if the judge says "Great argument, Counselor Kaling, the court concurs"—you also just want to not have to plead your case all the time. I wanted to be the judge, jury, and executive producer. (See what I did there?)

Here is a taste of the judge-versus-attorney dynamic between Paul and me in the final years at *The Office*.

Paul would give me an assignment, and if I didn't like it, sometimes I would still do it . . . but sometimes I would do something else. Then I would turn it in and wait for Paul to read it, hoping he would come out of his office, full of wonder and appreciation at my risk taking. "Mindy, I'm amazed by you," he would say, awestruck. "Not only did you complete the assignment, you *reinvented* the assignment. You reinvented comedy. Go home. Sleep the sleep of the creatively righteous."

Instead this is what happened.

PAUL: Hey. This is not the assignment I gave you.
ME: I didn't believe in the assignment you gave me, so I tried something else, and I'm pretty excited about the results, if I may say so—
PAUL: (*exasperated*) I don't care if you don't believe in it, go do it.

I can't imagine how difficult I was to manage back then. I don't think Paul could even have imagined it. I still don't think he believes it. He may have made it into a repressed memory that won't come out until after years of therapy.

The truth is, if I had a writer on my staff now who behaved like I did, I would throw them out the window of the writers' room, move their parking space to Structure C (it's really far away), and make them write 1,000 Morgan Tookers "when I was in prison" jokes.

Though I deserved it probably dozens of times, Paul never actually fired me. (Or, if he did, I never found out about it, because we have the same manager.)

The flip side to our fighting was the fact that I really loved working for him, because he was—and is—one of the most gifted writers I know. He was also a great leader. Methodical and soft-spoken,

Paul talked so quietly that sometimes I couldn't hear him when I was sitting next to him. I was always leaning in and saying "Huh? Heh?" It wasn't until later that I realized Paul's quietness was a result of his confidence. He didn't need to shout to be heard. I don't have that kind of confidence. My voice is loud and piercing, and I project like I was once told by a doctor during a childhood illness that I would never speak again. Anyone in a mile radius of our studio recognizes the brittle squawk of Mindy Kaling.

I noticed, though, as the years went by, that my passionate arguments became quieter. Part of me attributed it to my maturing and chilling out, but I suspected it might also be something a little more sad. I worried that my well of ideas for what could happen to this group of people working at a small paper company in Scranton, Pennsylvania, was going dry. That feeling was also making me antsy.

Over the course of the series, I had gone from a gleeful and inexperienced writer who couldn't believe she was in front of a camera to a pretty confident actress. The reason is because I went to the best comedy acting program in the world: the Steve Carell School of Acting. *The Office* was like sitting through a seven-year master class on comic acting led by Steve. At the Steve Carell School of Acting, I saw Steve get handed a page-long monologue, glance at it for twenty seconds, and have it memorized. He could go from craft services, where he could be enjoying a cup of tea and telling a funny story, to set, where, on cue, he could begin weeping like a faucet. When the director said cut, he would go back to his cup of tea and funny story. I once witnessed him make a room full of actors burst into laughter during a scene by improvising the line: "All right, everybody in the conference room! I don't care if you are gay or straight or a lesbian or overweight! Just get in here, right now!" For letting me watch him do all those things, I really ought to send him some money, but, honestly, he doesn't need it. He has that sweet *Despicable Me* money.

I told my manager, Howard Klein, privately how I felt, and so, at the end of season 7, when my original contract with Universal expired, they hired me to stay on as a writer and actress with *The Office*, and included a development deal for a pilot. A development deal is pretty rad. I got an assistant, whose job it was to figure out how iCloud worked and pretend to be my friend sometimes but let me yell at her other times. Basically I got a chunk of money to keep working on *The Office* but also to create a brand-new show, which I would write on Sunday afternoons sitting cross-legged on my bedroom floor with no pants on.

My natural assumption was that NBC would put my show on the air as part of a revitalized Must-See TV and make two hundred classic episodes—no lazy clip shows—finishing with a ninety-minute finale that everyone agreed was a sweet and satisfying send-off. I would emerge from the show's legacy as a modern version of Larry David and Mary Tyler Moore, retiring to a tasteful megacompound on Martha's Vineyard, where I would write plays and drink wine with Ted Danson and Mary Steenburgen at least several nights a week.

The one thing I was unprepared for was the slightest setback. What could go wrong?

"THE UNTITLED MINDY KALING PROJECT"

Let's go over my plan: I was going to write a show starring myself and it was going to be a smash hit. I would take everything good I learned at *The Office* and lose everything I didn't like about *The Office*. Mindy Kaling + Office good – Office bad = Best show ever made = Me someday receiving a Kennedy Center Honor from President Elizabeth Warren.

But first I had to assemble all of the ingredients I knew a great show had to have.

Ingredient #1: A Big Funny Lead

I knew I wanted my character in the new show to be a big comedy character. There are plenty of shows on TV where the lead female exists solely to be the calm, responsible voice of reason. She is often the one keeping the cast of kooky side characters at bay, saying stuff like "Guys, are you sure this is a good idea?" or "You guys go on the road trip to recover the sex tape; I'll stay here on the B-story about getting locked in the pantry."

My favorite shows have a flawed and ridiculous lead who is steering the comedy of the show, making big mistakes and then struggling to fix them. Basil Fawlty from *Fawlty Towers* was my favorite example, as was Edina Monsoon from *Absolutely Fabulous*, and Michael Scott, of course. This was a must.

Ingredient #2: A Compelling Setting

I wanted the audience to enjoy my character's bad behavior but also feel like she had some redeeming quality, which is the sneaky reason I chose to make Mindy Lahiri a doctor. I felt like if she did terrible things, but hey, she had this noble job where she was delivering babies and saving lives, people would respect her. This trick always works, by the way. That's why every doctor on TV is a drug addict, a sociopath, or just plain mega-rude. Doctors can do anything they want!

When I was first setting my new show in the world of doctors, I wanted the medical side of it to be front and center. It was my mother, an OB/GYN herself, who dissuaded me from that.

ME: Mom, let's talk about the practical details of your job, for research.

MOM: No, that is boring. If people want to see medical stuff they
     should watch *ER*.
ME: Mom, that show hasn't been on for years. Why shouldn't I
     put medical stuff in the show?
MOM: Because it's sad and even when it's happy, it can be grue-
     some.
MINDY: But shouldn't the show be gritty and realistic?
MOM: Here's realistic: when a baby is born, it's covered in blood
     and strange fluids. Occasionally it has a cord around its neck
     and it's blue and it's wailing because its little body is cold.
     The only people who think it's beautiful are its parents, and
     the doctor is just happy it's alive. And none of that is funny.

My mother had a great argument. Plus, I didn't want to hold
a prop baby covered in birth slime. If there were two things my
mom knew, it was comedy and obstetrics. And that was that.

Mom and I had always shared a love of romantic comedies and
the version of Manhattan that Nora Ephron and Woody Allen had
created for us in *You've Got Mail* and *Annie Hall*. She wanted me
to play a character in that world. She also wanted to see me in decent clothes for once. While she loved the comedy on *The Office*,
she also commented pretty regularly on how unglamorous it was.
"Mom, the show isn't supposed to be glamorous; it's supposed to
be real," I explained. "Like Greg always says: 'what's beautiful is
what's real.'"

"What's beautiful can also be what's beautiful, though," she
replied. "I think there has been some precedent of that in Hollywood." Not a bad point.

Mom continued, "I live real life every day. Why do I need to see
it when I come home?" How could I argue with that?

Ingredient #3: Literary Pretensions

The Mindy Project is most inspired by Jane Austen's *Pride and Prejudice*. Besides being in a structurally perfect novel, Elizabeth Bennet and Mr. Darcy are probably my favorite couple in any book.*
Danny Castellano is most based on Mr. Darcy (and a generous helping of Sonny Corleone from *The Godfather*). As for Mindy? Um, Mindy is much less like Elizabeth Bennet than she is a combination of Carrie Bradshaw and Eric Cartman.

Many people think romantic comedies are cheesy and boring, but that's only because most romantic comedies that come out now are less funny than, say, a card your grandmother might send you for your birthday. People also complain that romantic comedies are formulaic and the ending is always the same. So I *wasn't* going to do that.

Here's what my show would be like (the then-called *The Untitled Mindy Kaling Project*). Boy meets Girl. Boy hates Girl. Girl is not that crazy about Boy either. Eventually Girl wears Boy down with friendliness. Boy and Girl become confidants. Boy grows to love girl but can't express it. Boy and Girl get very close to marrying other boys and girls. Boy realizes he was being kind of a dick. Girl realizes she was being judgmental and superficial. Boy and Girl have sex. Boy and Girl accidentally get pregnant. Boy and Girl love each other as best they can and try to live happily ever after.

Let's see if that works!

QUICK AND PAINFUL REJECTION: SEE YA, NBC

I submitted *The Untitled Mindy Kaling Project* to NBC Studios on a Thursday before a weekend I had planned in Palm Springs

....
* Men! Psst, men! Are you still reading? Don't worry, we're past the chick-lit-girl-nerd stuff. Coming up next: competition, success, money, sex!

for my best friend Jocelyn's bachelorette party. I had heard there was some excitement about my script at the studio and assumed I would hear good news by the end of the workday on Friday. But as Saturday of that weekend rolled by, I still hadn't heard anything. Tipsy on margaritas and sleepy on poolside nachos, this was the first uneasy moment in which I considered the possibility that this pilot might not be a go. That night we went to a gay dance club, and while we were all dancing to Rihanna's "Rude Boy," I was starting to get worried.

It occurred to me that I barely knew the president of the studio at all, and this would be his decision entirely.

For the eight years that I had been there, NBC had been like a dysfunctional African country where the president changed every eleven months or so. Actually, NBC made most African countries look pretty stable by comparison. (Except Botswana. I hear good things about Botswana. That's where *The Ladies #1 Detective Agency* is.)

Over the entire run of *The Office*, there were seven different people who had run the studio and network. Bob Greenblatt was the newest chief. I had met him briefly at a party once; he was tall and elegant and red-haired. We were friendly, but we were not friends.

And now, trapped in Palm Springs, I thought: Oh fuck. Why am I only *friendly* with Bob Greenblatt? Why did I not force him to become my friend?!

By the end of Monday, I still had heard nothing. While shooting scenes for *The Office*, I heard from our writing staff about other pilots getting picked up to be filmed. For the first time in seven years in the TV business, I was completely terrified about my career.

Between lighting setups onstage, I called Howard, and my agent, Matt Rice, again. They were gentle, but the news was bad.

NBC had passed on my pilot. They didn't even like it—or me—enough to shoot it with no intention of ever picking it up! Where was my pity pilot? I told them I totally understood their decision (I didn't) and wasn't surprised (I was surprised), and hung up.

Then I sat in my trailer and wept.

When you are entitled, you are the most insufferable person ever. If you are entitled and hardworking, which I am, you are still pretty insufferable, but at least you somewhat earned your entitled behavior. For all my other theoretical faults, no one can deny my powerful and driven work ethic, handed down to me from my immigrant parents and my suburban Boston peer group of kids who thought Cornell was a safety school. I had thought it went without saying that I would one day have a show on NBC. It felt like destiny. It's crazily presumptuous, but I always imagined a world where my show was on the same network as my favorite Must-See TV shows. And now it wasn't going to happen.

It's weird when you feel your dream slipping away from you. Especially when you have no other dreams. I was surprised that my overwhelming feeling was not sadness; it was terror. What on earth am I going to do now? I thought. *The Office* isn't going to last forever. Would it end, and would I go work on a lesser comedy, sitting bitterly in the corner of the rewrite room of *My Mismatched Moms*, eating a California Pizza Kitchen Thai Crunch Salad with peanut dressing on the side, telling people how great *my* show would have been? Or would I have to take a job as the obligatory ethnic host of *House Hunters International*, my voiceover gamely trying to maintain the tension of "Which house will the couple pick?" when everyone knows it's the one the wife wants near the beach that's perfect for entertaining?

I had reached the level of self-obsessed insanity at which point no reasonable person would ever feel sorry for me. But sometimes, in life, or at least in driver's ed, the best advice is to "steer into the curve." It was from this terror that I got an idea. I remembered the man who had been the president of NBC when *The Office* first started. The man who greenlit *The Office* when no one else thought it could succeed and, later, *30 Rock*. That man was Kevin Reilly.

KEVIN REILLY, THE ONLY JOCK WHO HAS EVER LIKED ME

Kevin Reilly likes to speak in sports analogies. It's one of the most unsettling things about him because I am a nerd who doesn't understand anything sports-related at all, except Serena Williams's tennis outfits, which are fierce as hell. Kevin's always saying things like "You've got a real deep bench, now, kid." Or "You gotta keep your eye on the ball, and you're going to push it over the goal line." And I have no idea what he is talking about, but I nod enthusiastically and say, "Sure, of course, sports," and hope he doesn't ask any follow-up questions.

Kevin Reilly was always somewhat of a celebrity to me because, as I said, he had greenlit my favorite shows. His championing of *The Office* was particularly noteworthy because, at that time, critics and audiences alike weren't crazy about it. He just trusted Greg and Steve and knew it was worth standing by.

Kevin is also very, very handsome. Ridiculously handsome. He looks like the guy they'd cast to play "Network Executive" on a terrible but fun-to-watch TV show. More important, I really liked what Kevin liked. Network executives usually have bad taste. It's either just a reflection of what market research tells them that normal people are into, or whatever their adolescent children are obsessed with. I have so often been on the receiving end of whatever powerful network executive's children are watching that week. That is when I get calls telling me I should write an arc on my show for the singer Austin Mahone.*

Howard sent the pilot script to Kevin and he and his team read it immediately. I got a call that he would like to see me the following day.

Call me superficial, or call me a genius (or call me both—Why can't both be true?), but before the meeting, I went to the MAC store to get my makeup done, then to the Drybar on Sunset and got a blowout. I wanted Kevin and his team at Fox to see me as a potential star of a network TV show. They didn't need to see my large pores or my forty sad strands of witch hair. They wanted big, bouncy, shiny, *Two Broke Girls* hair!

I drove to the Fox lot across town, parked, drank two shots from a bottle of Jose Cuervo that I keep on the floor of my passenger seat, arranged my breasts so it looked like I had filled in a solid B-cup, dissolved enough Listerine breath strips on my tongue so the inside of my mouth was burning, and raced across the lot, hoping not to run into Rupert Murdoch in my Keds (I wear Keds to every meeting and then go the restroom and change into my "slutty career woman" stilettos before I actually see anyone important).

I was joined at the meeting by Bela Bajaria, the head of Universal Television Studios. I was very lucky that Bela was so supportive and determined to sell the show somewhere other than NBC. But she was also my boss, and her presence made me even more nervous. "You'll be great. You know what you're doing," Bela said warmly to me, a perfect stranger, while we waited to see Kevin. I nodded, grateful, while privately dying inside. How does she know I'll be great? I've never pitched a show before! I get nervous when I

....

* Austin Mahone (born April 4, 1996) is an American pop singer-songwriter. He is currently signed to Young Money Entertainment and Cash Money Records. He has filmed commercials for McDonald's and Hot Nuts, a Mexican snacking nut.

tell anecdotes! Sometimes I accidentally blurt out the ending right in the middle! Also, I'm sweating. Do great people sweat so much their thighs stick to the leather sofas they're sitting on?

I unstuck myself and we went into Kevin's office. The good news: Kevin was cheerful and open about how much he liked the script. His super-handsome face was glowing with handsome-ness. But he wasn't won over yet. He had some very specific notes he wanted me to address. The notes were about making sure that the character of Danny Castellano was strong and masculine. He didn't want my character to outsmart him and push him around. I had my assignment.

One of my very worst qualities is how impatient I am, but it's actually very helpful when I am rewriting. I skipped out of the Fox lot, threw my Keds back on, resisted the temptation to go over to the Simpsons building and take selfies with the Bart Simpson topiary, and raced to the car to take another shot of Cuervo for my drive home—this time a celebratory one.

For the next three days I worked nonstop. There is a certain type of greasy hair that you get only when you are writing with no breaks, and I had it, big-time. If I breathed in deeply, I could smell my unwashed scent and it was intoxicating. It smelled like hard work. You know on *Game of Thrones* how Khal Drogo always looked powerful and dirty because he'd been marauding nonstop for weeks? That's how I pictured myself. I was Khal Drogo on this pilot. My fingers were my Dothraki Khalasar. And Kevin Reilly was my Khaleesi, for I was going to make him/her mine/Drogo's.

I turned in the script to Bela and the rest of studio. They signed off on it and sent it to Kevin. I waited.

Two days later, Kevin called me. He said he wanted to shoot it.

Kevin didn't even use a sports metaphor, like "I'm putting your script into the game," he just said it. But in truth, my Hail Mary pass had been caught in the end zone just as the last seconds ticked off the clock. I just looked up those terms online.

I was so excited, and I was really scared. I no longer worked at *The Office*. I was going to have a new office. *My* office.

THE NO-LONGER-UNTITLED MINDY PROJECT/ THE TITLED MINDY PROJECT

Originally, in my pilot script, I had named my character Mira. But Kevin Reilly told me to change it to Mindy. This made me nervous. Ultimately, the note was the best advice (OK, order) that he ever gave me. By having the lead character share my name, it lent an authenticity to the show that people really responded to. Jerry Seinfeld kept his first name Jerry in *Seinfeld*, and it made you feel like you were his pal too, and that he wasn't trying to add distance between the viewer and his point of view. Calling her Mindy also inadvertently helped to make me more famous. My real name was on TV listings and billboards and radio ads across the country! Now whenever I see a subway ad for *The Mindy Project*, I can't believe it's my *actual name* on there, and I get so excited, even if my face has been vandalized with a Hitler mustache. Because that's how you truly know you've made it.

I had finally done it. I had created a show. Not for Must-See TV, home of *Cheers* and *Friends*. But for Fox, home of *Married . . . with Children* and *Joe Millionaire*. You never quite get everything you want the way you want it. But here I was, a showrunner and TV star, so who cared? Nothing bad would happen to me now. The end!

NOT SO FAST, BIG SHOT

Four years later, after three seasons, Fox canceled *The Mindy Project*. The day it was canceled, I was in Montana, on the first vacation I had taken in seven years. When I heard the news about the show, I was floating down the Blackfoot River. I was incredibly surprised. But I probably shouldn't have been. A year earlier, handsome, supportive, sports-analogy-using Kevin Reilly had left Fox for TBS, and the new heads of Fox did not agree with him that I was a valuable "designated hitter." You know when an old prewar building in Manhattan is bought by a developer and all the new tenants are cool yuppies, except there's one old rent-control crone left over from the Depression? And the landlord really wants to evict her but because of tenant rights has to pretend like "No, we love Crelga; she's so colorful and full of attitude. I love her Depression stories!," but secretly they are thinking of ways to have her replaced by John Stamos? It was kind of like that. I was Crelga.

The day we were canceled, I received hundreds of texts and emails, and *The Mindy Project* trended on Twitter. I have never been prouder of the show. We also received calls from other outlets that were interested in buying it. One was from the streaming platform Hulu. I knew Hulu because, besides sounding like a whimsical Danish candy, many of our fans were already watching it there. My friends Jason Reitman and James Franco were already doing series for them. Hulu was attracting better talent than the networks were, and when I met the president, Craig Erwich, he loved the show and wanted it to help establish their brand. Most important, though, he was good-looking. A week later, the deal was announced that Hulu had picked up *The Mindy Project* for season 4, for twenty-six episodes. I'd gone from barely having time to transition from my panic of not having a job to the panic of more work than I'd ever had before. And that's all show business is, really. Transitioning panics.

I think that's the lesson of this story: you never know what is going to happen.

Other lessons:

- No matter how good you have it, it's cool to want more.
- Self-pity gets results.
- Sometimes you can get a second chance.
- Sometimes you get a third chance.
- Never take a vacation.
- Austin Mahone has a bright future as a singer and youth-brand spokesperson.
- It's OK to drink tequila in the car if you just had a really good meeting.
- If you believe in yourself and work hard, your dreams will come true.
- Well . . . I guess the people who work hard whose dreams *don't* come true don't get to write books about it, so we never really find out what happens to them. So . . .
- If you believe in yourself and work hard, you have a fighting shot at having your dreams come true.

MINDY LAHIRI, MD, EVERYGIRL, MILD SOCIOPATH

EVERYONE KNOWS THAT ALL WHITE PEO-ple are racist. And the clearest evidence of that racism is when white people (as well as people of pretty much every other color) confuse *me* with the characters I write for myself to play. Racism: When will it end?

Between playing the selfish, boy-crazy narcissist Kelly Kapoor on *The Office* and the contrarian, delusionally confident Mindy Lahiri on *The Mindy Project*, I should probably give up on anyone thinking that I, Mindy Kaling, am normal or cool. But I still have hopes. So I thought I'd try to clear up some of the differences between the two Mindys. I did something similar with Kelly Kapoor in my last book, although I don't think anyone believed me.

Things Mindy Lahiri Would Do That I Would Not
- Dry her Spanx in an oven
- Send Michael Fassbender her underwear
- Own a gun and keep misplacing it
- Save a life
- Think Rick Santorum is hot

- Tell people she is twenty-four
- Have twelve handsome white boyfriends in one calendar year
- Sue a Boston Market for giving too-small helpings of sides
- Create a secret Twitter account just to follow the guys in One Direction and their fan accounts
- Deliver twins while wearing enough makeup for a *Vogue* cover shoot
- Flirt with a fireman while he was fighting a fire and be miffed she doesn't have his undivided attention
- Ask to board a plane early with parents and babies because she feels that she too "needs a little extra time to get settled"
- Get banned for life from Pinkberry for sample fraud

Things Mindy Lahiri and I Would Both Do
- Yell at teenagers for being too loud on the subway
- Graze at the Whole Foods hot foods bar and get reprimanded, then claim racism
- Go on dangerous juice cleanses
- Dress like a children's performer and think it's high fashion
- Say "Whoa" when we see a hot guy
- Say "Whoa" when we see a hot pizza
- Lie on the floor in despair a few times a year
- Have a fake phone conversation to avoid talking to the Über guy
- Explain to a person on a plane who doesn't speak any English the difference between Instagram and Pinterest
- Travel to the Super Bowl, but only for the parties the night before, and skip the game
- See food poisoning as an opportunity to springboard into a new exercise regimen
- Pretend not to have seen *Star Wars* to enrage *Star Wars* fans

ON BEING A MENTOR, BY GREG DANIELS

I KNOW WHAT YOU SEE WHEN YOU LOOK AT me. A powerful, self-realized woman of color with a brilliant mind and a body that won't quit. But I wasn't always this way. No, there was a time not long ago, when I was merely smart and hot. I'm so sorry, I'm obviously joking. But I guess there's some truth in every joke? So maybe it's kind of true?

I feel so lucky to have my career. But it was just over a decade ago that I was a scared twenty-four-year-old off-off-Broadway playwright trying to break in to TV writing with no connections in Hollywood. Not many people know me from back then, because I've had them all killed. Of the small handful of people still alive is my mentor, Greg Daniels.

Greg was the first person to hire me in Los Angeles, to work on *The Office*. You know when you meet someone so smart and cool that all their tastes and opinions seem like the correct ones? And you instantly think: those are my opinions now too! That's Greg to me. He would say he loved Monty Python and suddenly they were my favorite comedy troupe too. Most important, he took a chance on me, and he provided me with an example of someone whose career I admired and wanted.

The word *mentor* is funny because it has a pedagogical, formal feel to it. Greg never sat me down and said, "I believe in you, kid. Now, here, take this antique fountain pen that W. C. Fields gave me and go make something of yourself." He's always just provided opportunities for me, set an example of how to be a leader, invited me to his house for dinner sometimes, and sat in consoling silence across from me when I was going through heartbreak. He's wonderful.

I thought it might be interesting and useful to hear Greg talk about the experience of being a mentor and, if you're lucky, how he taught me how to be brilliant and gorgeous.

· · ·

MINDY ASKED ME to write a few words (actually 500 to 750, yikes) on "being a mentor, your philosophy on being a mentor, your relationship to me, your relationship to young women in your life, etc." So here goes:

What is a mentor? In scriptwriting, it's a character who teaches the hero something important, often dies at the act-two break, and provides that little extra bit of motivation the hero needs to climb tearfully over the mentor's broken body and *get it done!* No, thank you. Who wants to play that role in real life? The entertainment industry is swarming with talented young people who are willing to climb over your broken body and get it done. They are your competition and should be ruthlessly put down, not trained and encouraged. The most sensible response to reading a talented newcomer's spec script is to keep insisting, draft after draft, that it's confusing in some way, until they move back home and live with their parents.

Yet for some reason, I have been caught mentoring people. Why?

I blame having children. It messes with your instincts for self-preservation and substitutes a love of boring a captive audience that is forced to look up to you. And because I have daughters, I was particularly susceptible to Mindy's first message to me, conveyed through her agent, which was "Daddy, I need help with my math homework."

Actually, Mindy described our first meeting in her first book. In her depiction, I have the social skills of a Sasquatch, torturing her with long silences. In that interview, though, Mindy was really timid (bizarre, right?) and not showing the disco-ball light show that is her relaxed mind and that I was expecting after reading her spec script and seeing her stage show. So I gave her a lot of room to shine and open up. How could I have known that staring at her without speaking for minutes at a time didn't put her at ease? I'm not some mind-reading Sasquatch who knows the right thing to say in every situation. By now it should be clear that I don't really know the definition of Sasquatch.

As a mentor, I brought some craft experience developed over hundreds of table reads and rewrites on previous shows that I worked on or ran, as well as all my grumpy prejudices and bitter show-biz feuds. In return, Mindy wrote hilarious jokes and fresh dialogue, which I put on the air with glee. Whether by giving notes on her outlines and scripts, cowriting Jim and Pam's wedding, or pitching out a new animated show (still one of my favorite yet-to-be-produced projects ever), collaborating with Mindy is a joy.

I have had the benefit of a lot of great mentors, starting with Lorne Michaels and Jim Downey at *Saturday Night Live*, and including Jim Brooks, David Mirkin, and Al Jean and Mike Reiss at *The Simpsons*. I know a lot of people are probably thinking, good for you, but nobody has ever wanted to be *my* mentor. You take your mentoring where you can find it, even if it is not being offered to you. Have you ever used your neighbor's Wi-Fi when it wasn't on a password? If you have the opportunity to observe someone at work, you are getting mentoring out of them even if they are unaware or resistant. Make a list of the people you think would make the greatest mentors and try to get close enough to steal their Wi-Fi. I wrote a freelance *Seinfeld* episode for Larry David; I can't say he took any interest in my welfare, but I was able to watch him work and pick up stuff. That's what drew me to meet with Ricky Gervais and Stephen Merchant. They were practitioners of my chosen craft at the highest level possible, and if I had to pretend to be interested in adapting *The Office* for the United States in order to meet them, then so be it.

OK, I'm at about 660 words so far, and I haven't even addressed "your relationship to young women in your life." By the way, have you noticed what a shameless fishing expedition that question is? She just throws it in at the end of a list like I'm going to slip up and confirm my vacationing with Ariana Grande. We were photographed in the same airport lounge, OK? If there had been enough seats, she wouldn't have been sitting on my lap. Just two random travelers killing time by hooking up. No big deal.

I LOVE SEX SCENES!

I N HOLLYWOOD, I AM CONSIDERED A PRUDE. Perhaps the main reason is that I'm not a comedian who speaks frankly about my sexuality, making me the only woman in Hollywood who is not speaking frankly about her sexuality. You can't walk down the street or be on any social media platform for more than nine seconds before an actress mentions how it's imperative that she and everyone else "free the nips." If you don't know what I'm talking about, please Google it. You wouldn't believe me if I explained it here. This is the world I live in.

People may also think I'm a prude because my television show, though about dating and romance, is not really about sex, like, say, *Sex and the City* was. That's because my show is on a major network and you can't show all that stuff, and also because my dad is alive and I would like to have lunch with him without feeling mired in dishonor.

The truth is I'm a weird mix of fearful New England prig and repressed pervert. On the one hand, I think sex is private and special, and I would rather die than ever write or talk about my sex life in any public way. And on the other, I am an unabashed lover of watching sexy situations on-screen, both as a viewer and, lately, as a participant on my own show.

My buddy Mark Duplass opening the door without a shirt on for a sexy interaction

So, there must be lots of other actors who love doing sex scenes too, right? Wrong. If you interview any actor about having to do sex scenes, you always get the same answer: they "hate" doing them.

It's actually kind of annoying; you're there for twelve hours; it's exhausting. —Justin Timberlake

There's like one hundred and fifty crewmen watching and you see each other's bits and pieces. The whole thing is just wrong.
—Mila Kunis

They're hard to do. You're doing things that you're supposed to do with only certain people in your life. —Kerry Washington

I am here to tell you that they are all lying. Every last one of 'em. Obviously, on-screen sex is not actual penetrative sex, but as any religious high-schooler will tell you, simulating sex can be pretty damn enjoyable as well.

And why shouldn't it be? You get to crawl around in a bed with another person you either a) already know really well or b) are getting to know better in the most cozy and intimate way possible. Yes, it is true that an entire room of people is watching you when you shoot a sex scene. To that, I say: the more, the merrier! Most of those people are artists whose job it is to make sure your physical imperfections are cloaked in mysterious shadows. By the end of the shooting day, you'll wish there were *more* people there.

MINDY KALING, TONGUE BANDIT

Earlier this year I realized that, for a long time, I had been completely breaking the rules of stage kissing. I learned that among professional actors the tacit rule of on-screen kissing is "open mouth, no tongue." In 1985, during the AIDS crisis, the Screen Actors Guild even made this their official policy. I, however, became a professional actor on *The Office* at the height of my early-twenties boy craziness, and the only person I was kissing was my best friend, B. J. Novak. We did not stage kiss because we didn't know any better. It was just lights, camera, tongue-dance.

Anders Holm and I make out naked in a shower
with thirty people standing two feet away.

So when I created *The Mindy Project* and I was suddenly acting in all these romantic situations, it never occurred to me to ask my scene partners if they minded tongue kissing. I just kissed as I would kiss naturally, and they always reciprocated. If they were psyched or felt bullied, I will never know, because no one ever mentioned it to me as an issue. So, if my math is correct, I have broken SAG rules about twenty-one times. And you know what? If they take away my SAG card because of it, I can only say: it was worth it.

THE SEXIEST THING THAT HAS EVER HAPPENED TO ME

I've had the privilege of making out with dozens of actors on camera. Once I had to do a particularly involved make-out with an actor who happens to be a married acquaintance of mine. The shot was complicated and the director spent hours shooting it over and over. The sheer number of takes made me feel self-conscious about my ability to make out in an authentically sexy way. Between takes, in a moment of insecurity, I turned to my scene partner and whispered: "God, this is taking forever. Am I doing this terribly?"

He looked me in the eye, took my hand, and gently guided it to the front of his pants where I felt the unmistakable presence of an erection. My jaw dropped. He winked at me, said, "I think you're doing just fine," and dropped my hand.

We never spoke of it again. It is, to this day, the sexiest thing that has ever happened to me.

WHY ALL ACTORS MUST LIE

So why are all your favorite actors and actresses lying about enjoying sex scenes? Well, a couple of reasons:

1) *Creepiness.* Anyone who announces they love filming sex scenes is going to be perceived as some kind of weirdo who gets

their jollies off at work. No one wants to act with them, as honest (and, frankly, as entertaining) as they sound.

2) *Vulnerability*. People don't like to admit they loved shooting a sex scene, because, like sex, what if the other person didn't like it that much? I once complimented my friend Seth Rogen on his on-screen kissing skills. Then later, while we were waiting during a lighting setup, I shyly asked him what he thought of mine, and he took a moment to think, and replied: "To be honest, I don't really remember." That's what Seth Rogen thinks of my kissing. So good he didn't remember it *fifteen minutes later*.

Seth Rogen: Great kisser, nice energy, beard not too scratchy

3) *Significant Others*. Actors are the only people in the world who are allowed to essentially stray from their marriages physically and *there are no repercussions*. Zero. In fact, if they're especially good at sex scenes, thousands of people will want to steal them away. If you are the unlucky spouse of an actor, the last thing you want to hear is that, in addition to him getting to fake-cheat on you by virtue of the most unfair loophole of all time, he also really enjoyed it.

4) *Integrity*. In kabuki times, actors were literally prostitutes, and we have spent centuries trying to distance ourselves from that profession. Occasionally we have setbacks, like *The Bachelor* and *The Bachelorette*. But in general, it's very important for us not to seem like we are being financially compensated for sex acts. People already think acting is the world's easiest and most frivolous

job, besides Miss Golden Globe. So we all have this tacit agreement to keep our traps shut about the world's best job perk.

That is why I, a noted Hollywood bad boy with nothing to lose, must be the person to tell the truth. Sex scenes are the tits. You're welcome.

COMING THIS FALL

ᘒᘒ

I'VE BEEN IN THE TELEVISION BUSINESS FOR eleven years, which is a very long time. Not long by regular-job standards, but, at thirty-five, people around here are beginning to call me seasoned. "Seasoned," for those of you not in show business, is the worst insult you can call a woman. It means a cross between "old," "disagreeable," and "only wears slacks." TV is a young man's game, like professional sports. And after eleven years, you're not the rookie, you're the old guy in the dugout talking about the old days and spitting into a tin can. That last part is the only part I actually do.

Every pilot season, the trade papers all publish loglines of the upcoming pilots that are going to be shot. I now can see certain tropes get recycled over and over. I'm not just referring to familiar characters you've come to expect on most shows (for example "boozy mother-in-law," "candid black best friend," "hyper-articulate child of dum-dums," and "incomprehensible foreigner"). I'm talking about premises for entire series that seem to get reused perennially.

Much like my love for romantic comedies, I enjoy most television. I could only make this list because I have watched more TV than an angry thirteen-year-old child of divorce. The only thing I will not watch is reality television. "Watch how we pick a singer!" "Watch how we turn this old crappy house into a cool new one!" No, *you* do that! I don't need to see the process. I *live* the process. Let me relax.

Here are the kinds of shows that networks seem to be clamoring for lately.

BOY-MAN MUST FACE THE ADULT WORLD

Carter can't keep a job. His girlfriend left him for smoking too much pot. His dog ran away because he never went outside. He high-fives his African American roommate while they play Xbox. He lives in filth. He sometimes wears his pants inside out. This is the story of how he became the attorney general of the United States of America.

THE STAUNCH OVAL OFFICE DAME

This briskly paced show centers on our heroine, a tough, highly educated woman in a high-pressure job full of gross, sexist men. She is the very best person at her job, and she is so moral she would send her own husband to the electric chair if he was found guilty of shoplifting. But she harbors a terrible, humiliating, dark secret: she's *dyslexic*. And, in the world of this show, that could get her impeached.

POOR MARIA

This is the charming tale of a lovely Latina "regular looking" girl (that is, she would be considered a perfect "10" if she were white). She has a heart of gold but is underestimated by everyone around her . . . except the handsome white CEO of the corporation where she sweeps the floors. Will he whisk her away like the dust particles in her bin? Or will he fire her when he finds out she is part of the Floor-Sweeping Union that wants their salaries to be raised to $4 an hour?

REMAKE OF GRITTY ISRAELI SHOW ABOUT TERRORISTS/INFIDELITY/MENTAL ILLNESS

This well-produced and depressing show will be the one you know you should be watching but just can't make yourself do it. Let's examine the best case here. You invest the time watching the show, you mention it at a party, and some guy tells you how much better the original Israeli version was. Ditto for British comedies about the workplace.

DAD! MOM!

You know that thirty-eight-year-old guy in your office who falls to pieces when his seventy-year-old parents get a divorce? Then Dad moves in and has to learn Internet dating? And Son reverts to behavior he did when he was ten! No? Well, you're the only one, because there are usually five pilots about this very subject at any given time at every network.

THE ABANDONED SPINSTER CLUB

A confident workaholic woman named Marcia or Alex comes home to find her husband cheating on her in her own bed with his secretary. It's always the middle of the afternoon and it's always happening in her own bed. I find this little detail especially horrifying. It's bad enough that it's happening, but we need to wring out as much humiliation as we possibly can. "You know what would make the cheating even *worse*? If it were happening in her own bed *next to photos of their kids and stuff.*"

The rest of the series explores her journey to accepting a new life as a sex-positive fortysomething. She will have a really fun assistant who's an expert on all the new, slutty dating techniques. Also, everyone on this show drinks wine while sitting on couches. And they're in jeans and barefoot with one foot tucked under them. Think about it.

HOT SERIAL KILLER WHO'S KIND OF LITERARY

He leaves sonnets pinned to all the corpses. The murdered prostitutes all have the first names of Jane Austen heroines. The kindly police commissioner's name is Chuck Dickens. The whole thing takes place in a tough housing project in Newark called Stratford-up-by-Avon. A melancholy English actor plays the lead in this mystery drama, and he uses his accent no matter what country it takes place in. This is everyone's mom's favorite show.

NEUROTIC SENSITIVE GUY IS ALSO SUPER UNHAPPY

Usually a half-hour cable comedy show. This wealthy L.A.- or NYC-based man, who makes his living doing something creative, is miserable despite having suffered no traumas or having any immediate health problems. If there are kids, they are only invoked to interfere with sex life. The pilot will always involve a child's birthday party with a bouncy house, or a clown who breaks character when not around the kids. Deemed brilliant and hilarious, this show usually has no jokes.

SUPERHERO: BEFORE!

You know that famous superhero with his own franchise of block-buster movies? He's great, isn't he? Wouldn't you like to know what he was like when he was a kid, way before his cool powers took effect? No? OK, how about what his mom and dad were like? No, they don't have any superpowers. It's just an awesome, talky prequel, with lots of prophetic talk about what will happen in those movies you love so much.

TALKATIVE CHUBSTER SEEKS HUSBAND

A sexually unapologetic fashionista tries to find love in the big city . . . wait a second! This sounds like the premise of *my* show, *The Mindy Project*. But it's not my fault. I didn't come up with this format. Not many people know this, but *The Mindy Project* is actually based on a famous Venezuelan show called *Puta Gordita*, or "The Chubby Slut."

A DAY IN THE LIFE OF MINDY KALING

F OR THE PAST ELEVEN YEARS, I HAVE LIVED the life of a vampire. Starting with *The Office*, my dual jobs as a comedy writer and an actor required me to wake up before the sun has risen, return home after the sun had set, and pace around in windowless rooms all day. Were I not dark-skinned, my skin would be translucent and pale like a vampire's. Also, I drink human blood for beauty reasons.

Then, when I created my own show, *The Mindy Project*, it just got more pronounced. I had to arrive earlier to set in the morning, stay later at night, and work on the weekends. It's a subterranean life for mole people, but as we all know, mole people have exciting and sexy lives. Sure, there are moments of panic and occasional bouts of crying, but there's also the joy of creating something I love. And since I don't have kids yet, I don't have the guilt of leaving them to come to work every day. Ha-ha, working mothers! Suck on my callow existence! I also did that thing that corrupt politicians do where I hired all my friends to work with me, so that's very nice as well. I like to think of myself as the Rod Blagojevich of television.

"What exactly do you do all day?" people ask me. I think the perception to many is that I sit all day in a candy-colored office surrounded by giggling tweens, where we compare whale-tails and prank-call boys, not unlike Katy Perry's video for "California Gurls." I wish that were my life, but sadly it's not. I would love to have Snoop Dogg waiting in my office in a cupcake-print suit to tell all my problems to. Wouldn't we all?

To help describe what it's like, I thought I would show you, for a picture is worth a thousand words (and, as it turns out, a lot easier than writing a thousand words).

5:00 a.m.

No, this is not a still from *Paranormal Activity*. This is what I look like while I'm sleeping just before my five a.m. alarm. I had my brave assistant Sonia trail me for a few days to document my goings-on. Yes, I am a little worried that these photos are on her phone. No, I didn't do a background check when I hired her at the bus station. Guys, relax! Sonia's chill and loves God. That's what her tattoos say.

5:07 a.m.

Here you can see my daily ritual of lolling in bed for an extra five to seven minutes, delaying the inevitable. This is a portrait of me at my most miserable.

5:15 a.m.

Ah, here we have some naked early-morning showering, just a little something to keep you perverts interested.

5:45 a.m.

Now I begin my drive in the dark from West Hollywood to Universal Studios. I have seen some fascinating examples of humanity in these hours. Meth heads arguing in the parking lot of a Kumon, a man pleasuring himself on a bus-stop bench. Years ago I would've called them creeps. Now I call them my commute buddies.

6:00 a.m.

I report to the hair and makeup trailer, where, suddenly, I am completely awake and very chatty. My morning chattiness is not reciprocated by very many other actors I've ever worked with. I don't get it at all. Who wouldn't like to experience the sun

rising to a monologue about Khloe Kardashian's line of girdles? Adam Pally and Chris Messina like to remain silent in the hours of six a.m. to eight a.m., which is excruciating to me. B. J. Novak is famously grumpy in the morning. After years of morning fights, I finally came up with the brilliant idea of doing a "B.J. coffee check," where I would peer into his cup of coffee to see how much of it he had drunk. I would not even attempt to talk to him until it was more than two-thirds done.

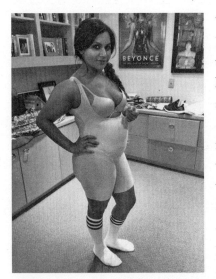

7:00 a.m.

Now I must put on my costume. Sometimes, it's a chic layered outfit featuring designers such as Oscar de la Renta or Marni. Other times, it's a pregnancy fat suit. At the end of season 3, Mindy was pregnant, but when you are a size 10, you're not super excited about wearing extra padding all day. For vanity reasons, I wanted to be the world's most svelte expectant mother, so I asked my costume designer, Sal, for the "Bethenny Frankel special." He said no. What does a pregnancy pad feel like? It feels like wearing Spanx stuffed with a spongy foam pumpkin. Great! Love it! There are no small parts, there are only plump actors who dislike pregnant parts.

7:45 a.m.

Today we are shooting an episode with American treasure Stephen Colbert. He plays a Catholic priest and former drug and sex addict who once did it with Madonna on an airport baggage carousel. I like to take beloved television icons and have them say terrible things on camera for laughs. Peabody this, Colbert.

8:00 a.m.

One of the responsibilities of being a writer-performer is that after I rehearse with the other actors, I make adjustments to the script on the fly. Here's director Michael Spiller, writer

Tracey Wigfield, and me talking through the lines and looking for places we could make changes. Michael's probably saying something like "This is perfect, I don't see how you could improve *any* of it! Go to craft services and treat yourself to a doughnut."

8:20 a.m.

I have two writer-producers on set, the likable Midwestern writing team of Ike Barinholtz and David Stassen. Ike plays Nurse Morgan, and it surprises people that he's a writer, because Morgan

is an ex-con who pronounces the word "intelligence" with a hard *g*. Ike and Dave's job is to write alts, run them in to the actors on set, and wear matching gingham shirts. For two sweet, well-raised men, their jokes can be breathtakingly raunchy. But at their core, they are old-fashioned Chicago gentlemen who will always open a door for you or eat seventy buffalo wings with you.

Noon

At noon we break on set for lunch. I take a golf cart over to the writers' building, which is across the lot. I drive my golf cart like a pro, which is yet another way I resemble an old white man.

This is the insane asylum where I was raised. Just kidding! This is *The Mindy Project* production office. Our writers' room is on the third floor of *The Mindy Project* building. The other two floors house our accounting, locations, clearance, set-design, and art departments. They are all hardworking people with fantastic candy bowls.

Even though the building only has three floors, I have never once taken the stairs. Yes, we have an elevator for a building with three floors, because this is Los Angeles, where we all drive two blocks to run on a  treadmill for forty-five minutes. Once I'm in the writers' room, I interrupt all productivity because I haven't seen my writing staff yet and I am starved for gossip. Usually the gossip is "meh," like my writer Chris might say he and his boyfriend were at brunch and saw Cat Deeley. But I'll take it! Then Matt Warburton, an executive producer, goes through what the writers are working on so I can weigh in. Then I bark, "This is all terrible! Start over!," even if it's good. It's been proven that writers are funnier when they are demoralized.

For lunch I usually have something hearty like a burger or tacos. I have always believed lunch should be the biggest meal of the day. People who say breakfast should be the biggest meal are insane. You can't have dessert at breakfast.

12:25 p.m.

I'm fanatical about brushing my teeth after lunch. My show is about dating, so you never know when you are going to kiss someone. That's the kind of sexy, unpredictable set I like to run. Oh! I need to mention here that the behavior and opinions expressed in this essay are those of the author and do not reflect the official policy or position of Universal Television Group.

12:30 p.m.

Once a week, Matt, a couple of other writers, and I hop on a conference call with executives to pitch them the story for an upcoming episode. I explain the key points of the story, and, afterward, I get reactions from everyone on the call. Sometimes I mute the call and make exasperated and/or disrespectful comments.

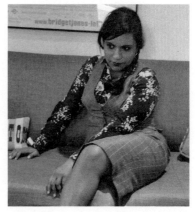

1:00 p.m.

After lunch is when we hold our table read for the next episode. I love table reads because it's like a mini live performance and the energy reminds me of when I did plays back in New York. Also,

the space between the wall and the table is very small, so sometimes handsome actors have to hold on to me to squeeze by.

Knowing which jokes play well is so important to us that one of the assistants' entire job at the read is to listen carefully and put a check mark next to a place where there was a laugh. Nothing is sadder than pages of unmarked dialogue.

2:00 p.m.

Now it is time to get beautified again to go act. In the hours since I arrived on set, I now have an oily face, hair snarls, and food particles in clothes. A fleet of fashionably dressed women clean all that up so America doesn't have to see any of it.

2:30 p.m.

And now, back to shooting.

3:15 p.m.

More shooting.

4:45 p.m.

Sometimes during the day there is a birthday in the writers' room, so I will scurry over for a quick round of "Happy Birthday," jam some cake in my mouth, and head back to set. It's important to make a big deal about birthdays at work because we spend so many hours here, and enormous amounts of food makes you miss your family less.

5:00 p.m. and throughout the day

Around five p.m. and later, I get very silly. Ike and I have a terrible habit of setting each other off on laughing fits, or "breaking," that makes it impossible to continue to shoot the show, and it's worse in the afternoon because my tiredness is starting to set in. It can sometimes be a line of dialogue, but usually it's something tiny: an especially belabored sigh, a little facial twitch, the way one of us chooses to plop down in a roller chair. I've even lost it by the way that Ike puts his glasses on. This happens about once a week and lasts seven to ten minutes. These are some of my favorite times with him and on set.

If I am lucky, at least once an episode we have some kind of party or birthday scene and I get to eat cake on camera. Prop cake is the sweetest kind of cake because, unlike with regular cake, it has no calories because my *character* is eating it, not me. That's how it works. Also, I am *getting paid to eat cake*. It's a Two-Caker Day when it's a writer's birthday and cake is called for in a scene—a day as rare and wonderful as Halley's Comet.

5:30 p.m.

During another set-up, I take my golf cart over to the soundstage, where I do ADR, which stands for additional dialogue recording. That's the disembodied voice you hear at the beginning of an episode. Such as this:

MINDY (voiceover)

It's so great to be back in New York in the winter. Curling up in a warm bed next to the one you love. The only problem is, I'm pregnant and morning-sick as hell.

6:00 p.m.

Getting in a quick nap. I sleep so deeply, and so quickly, my writer Tracey Wigfield has commented that when I close my eyes to nap, "It's like you die for a few minutes."

6:15 p.m.
More shooting.

8:00 p.m.

When we are shooting, I am always able to find creative places to take quick naps. Eleven years into this, I am able to sleep through any amount of noise and temperature. Sometimes I wake up and hope I slept through a *Walking Dead*–type zombie apocalypse and I have to lead humans into a new world order.

8:15 p.m.

I am wrapped on set! It's not like you see in plays and movies where someone yells "That's a wrap!" and then the cast all changes into street clothes and grabs their backpacks and goes to a local bar.

When we wrap, everyone tears off their costumes and races home to their neglected children, only to find they have begun to call the nanny "Daddy." I go to my trailer to look over my lines for the next day and accidentally call Sonia my wife.

8:30 p.m.

I then wash my face free of makeup and throw on my street clothes and re-join the writers for dinner. Our writers get along very well, but the fights we've had over what we should eat for dinner are the most acrimonious Lannister/Stark throwdowns I've ever been a part of.

9:30 p.m.

After the writers leave, I head to editing. Here is my quiet sanctuary, where it is just me, the editor, a bag of McDonald's, and the episode in front of me. "Let's make something really special," I say to my editor, Dave Rogers, who worked on *Seinfeld* and *The Office*. "Get your feet off the coffee table," he replies. We have fun.

12:30 a.m.

About 50 percent of the time, I have enough energy to remove my clothes and put on pajamas when I go to bed. Otherwise I just fall asleep in the clothes I went to work in, which I like to think of as a sexy, ongoing walk of shame.

And then I sleep and dream of birthday cakes to come, both fake and real.

BAD SPORT

I AM A TERRIBLE SPORT. BY AGE EIGHT, I HAD been banned from playing board games by my mother because of how competitive and intense I got. Relaxed after-dinner games of Monopoly deteriorated into tear-soaked affairs with accusations of cheating, favoritism, and veiled death threats. Extended family had to be apologized to; desserts were revoked.

I've chilled out a little as I've gotten older, but my "bad sport" streak still rears its head sometimes. Once, while living in New York City in the early 2000s, I was asked to leave a sports bar because the Yankees were playing my hometown Red Sox on TV and I lost my cool at a guy who was loudly dissing them. I yelled, "Derek Jeter is baseball's Hitler!" This was in *New York City*. In a room full of *Jewish sports fans*. I don't even really like baseball that much! I have problems.

In 2014, the Academy of Television Arts and Sciences asked me to announce the annual Emmy nominations. I was excited about it for one reason, and one reason alone: I thought, This might help me get nominated for an Emmy!

I should say here that although I love praise that is broadcast live to millions of people, receiving an Emmy nomination is not simply about the recognition. Any nomination, in any category, would help *The Mindy Project* enormously because, in a world where you are not getting huge ratings, every little bit of prestige helps to convince a network to keep you on the air. But also, I love praise broadcast to millions of people. And the helping-the-show thing.

The Emmy announcements take place at 5:30 a.m., Pacific Standard Time, because when we are finding out the top six contenders for best miniseries, movie, or dramatic special, it's important that the whole nation watch as one. I woke up at two a.m. and drove to the Academy building in North Hollywood. Contrary to what you might think, North Hollywood is not in Hollywood, or even that close to it. It's in the Valley. Actually, North Hollywood is to Hollywood as Newark is to New York; it really sounds like the other thing but it's way, way different, to the point where you're like, "Hey, man, are you trying to trick me? Because this place is *definitely* not like that other place." North Hollywood is actually kind of nice during the day, but it is not a place you want to be at 2:30 a.m. in stiletto heels. Once I got inside the Academy building, I sat in the green room getting my hair and makeup done during the time that, on any normal night, I would be dreaming about Idris Elba's and my honeymoon. (It's in the Seychelles, we fight on the first night, make up the next morning, and never fight again for the rest of our lives.)

Carson Daly was presenting with me, and he arrived at 3:30 a.m. and popped his head in to say hello. I know Carson a little, and I like him a lot. I always marvel at his schedule. He hosts *The Voice*, which shoots in Los Angeles, then cohosts the *Today* show, which shoots in New York City, and that's in addition to hosting *Last Call with Carson Daly*, which shoots in L.A. again. He seems to have this impossible schedule and *still* manages to be a funny and down-to-earth guy. Which means he is either a rare and wonderful person or he is twins who live on opposite coasts and have committed their lives to this low-stakes and marvelous hoax. I like either explanation.

We rehearsed on set at four a.m. Afterward, the president of the Academy, Bruce Rosenbaum, came by. He was very sweet, and greeted me, saying, "Hi, Mindy. Thanks for being here." I thanked him for inviting me. That's when it happened. Bruce looked away for a second, and his tone shifted ever so slightly. "You know, you're in *such* a tough category," he said kindly, patting my arm, then walked away to concern himself with other matters.

That's when I knew I wasn't going to get nominated. If I hadn't been paying close attention, I wouldn't have noticed it, but there it was, no mistake about it. Bruce was trying to tell me so I could prepare my reaction when I had to announce the news on live TV. The disappointment hit me fast, and it hit me hard. It wasn't until that moment that I realized how much I actually wanted it.

Did I think I deserved a nomination? I don't know, yeah! Maybe it sounds egotistical, but if you're a person who creates your own show and stars in it, shouldn't you believe you deserve recognition for it? If you don't, then why not? Worse yet, who will?

Then an even worse feeling quickly eclipsed my disappointment. I realized: Oh, no. Now I have to stand here on a stage in goddamn North Hollywood and announce these other people while everyone sees me not get nominated. I gave up Idris Elba honeymoon dream sex for this bullshit?

That's when that old familiar feeling began to surge inside my veins. Bad sport. Hurt ego. Not wanting to stay and watch while my family kept playing Monopoly after I had gone bankrupt because I kept landing on "jail" and couldn't buy my way out because I bought too many goddamn railroads and Dad wouldn't lend me money because it was against the rules!

ARGGHH!!! SCREW EVERYONE. I WANNA WIN!!!

Photos taken of me just before the announcement

I battled two instincts:

1) To bail on the whole event so I didn't have to read the names of a bunch of Poindexters whose shows I don't care about, which would cause a massive PR disaster, and I would be considered a "Charlie Sheen" type problematic personality from now on, or,

2) To stay and be gracious so people would continue to think I'm professional and classy.

Instinct number 2 won out. But not by much. If Carson only knew how close he was to having to read all those names by himself. Although, I bet his secret twin would've shown up and helped him. Ugh. They probably would have done it effortlessly and been the heroes of the whole morning.

We read the names live at 5:30 a.m. and I was very nervous. It was a strange kind of nervousness. Now that I knew I wasn't going to be nominated, I was nervous because everyone would be watching me, and I desperately needed to react in a calm and confident way when they *didn't* call my name. There are enough people out there who would *love* to see my face falter at that moment, make a GIF about it, give it a mean caption, and send it out to all their friends.

So I wasn't going to give it to them.

Before Carson read my category, "Lead Actress in a Comedy Series," I unfocused my eyes on the teleprompter, and I pictured myself in 2002, in Brooklyn, wishing I knew a way to break into Hollywood and thinking, with no hope at all, *There is no way out of this situation.* I was so innocent and naïve—I probably still thought North Hollywood was close to Hollywood. As Carson started reading names, I tuned him out and thought about how the only reason I was even asked to present that morning was because I was the star of a show that was considered relevant and attention-getting, and how that anxious twenty-two-year-old in Brooklyn would have slept so much better knowing I would be standing here one day. It had an oddly calming effect, and by the time Carson was reading the last nominee—Melissa McCarthy—I stood next to him, looking positively serene on camera. The greatest crime is that I wasn't nominated for *that* acting performance.

Carson and I finished the announcements; I stuck around for a few pictures and then bolted. The instant it was over I took off my heels, slipped sweatpants on under my dress, put on my glasses, and drove to the McDonald's on Sunset and Crescent Heights, where I ordered two Egg McMuffins, hash browns, and a large orange juice, and ate them all in the parking lot. With a little time to distance myself from it, I was surprised by how genuinely happy I was for the friends whom I had been able to announce nominations for, like Lizzy Caplan and Stephen Colbert. I was also proud of myself, a notorious bad sport, for being a gracious grown-up, something I have never been.

Of course, people still wrote articles. But because there was no story, they wrote these sad little pieces about how there was no story. One website published a piece called "Watch Mindy Kaling Keep It Together as She Announces Her Own Emmy Snub." I loved that one because it's basically "Watch Nothing Happen but I Have to Write Something Mean and Today Is a Slow News Day." After breakfast, I drove to work, where I have the best job in the world, lips greasy from my hard-earned McMuffin(s). I'm lovin' it (them).

Throwing a tantrum feels good because you think you are ruining everyone's good time when you feel your very worst. But the truth is, you're not ruining their good time, you're just giving them another good story. I would like to think this experience helped me to kick off a lifetime of grace and the ability to express happiness for people who are doing well when I am not. But I doubt I will always have a camera pointed at me, live, with millions of people watching to keep me honest. So we shall see.

Love, Dating, and Boys Who Ru(i)n the World

SOUP SNAKES

What really knocks me out is a book that, when you're all done reading it, you wish the author that wrote it was a terrific friend of yours and you could call him up on the phone whenever you felt like it. That doesn't happen much, though.

—HOLDEN CAULFIELD*

B. J. Novak and me, in 2004 (left) and 2014

'M VERY LUCKY. MY FAVORITE WRITER IS someone I can call up on the phone whenever I feel like it. That's because my favorite writer is my friend B. J. Novak.

....

* If quoting J. D. Salinger's *The Catcher in the Rye* right off the bat scares you, you're really not going to like when I reference *The Heart Is a Lonely Hunter* and *Animal Farm* later. Basically, I stopped reading after ninth grade. Just kidding! Just keep reading!

I will freely admit: my relationship with B.J. is weird as hell. He is not my boyfriend, but he is not exactly my best friend. The best way I would describe him is that he is my ex-husband, and we have a son who is away at boarding school, so our fighting can never get *that* bad, because it would upset our child. I don't think Facebook would accept that as a new status. They would just categorize it as "it's complicated."

The occasional way we've described our relationship is "soup snakes." This term comes from a season 7 episode of *The Office* where Michael Scott is reunited with his ex-girlfriend Holly and is pretending he doesn't have feelings for her anymore. Later, he privately confesses to camera:

MICHAEL

I wrote down a list of bullet points why Holly and I should be together, and I'm going to find the perfect moment today and I am going to tell her.

(Michael pulls out a ratty little piece of paper with writing scribbled all over it. He reads from it.)

Number one: Holly, you and I are . . . soup snakes. The . . . and the reason is . . . because . . . in terms of the soup, we like to . . . that doesn't make any sense. (*realizing he is misreading his own handwriting*) We're soul mates. Holly and I are soul mates.

I think I love the scene because it reflects how love works. "Soul mates" is what you aim for, but soup snakes is what you get sometimes.

I show B.J. everything I write. Though he generally loves my writing, he doesn't always love everything. And when he doesn't, I don't take it very well, which will come as a surprise to no one. When B.J. doesn't like something I write, I am deeply wounded, extremely mad, and vow to never show him anything again.

"Maybe you're just not the audience for this?" I respond icily, like I am a relevant, important female voice expressing myself and he is some out-of-touch Brooks Brothers shirt who can't handle my real-ness. "But thanks for your criticism. I'll take that into account." Exasperated, he'll respond, "I'm sorry, did you just want me to tell you how great it was?" Yes, I did, B.J.! Is that so horrible? People don't say "Give me your honest opinion" because they want an honest opinion. They say it because it's rude to say "Please tell me I'm amazing."

We hang up and don't talk to each other for a few days. Then he calls me to see if I want to go get sushi and watch *Gone Girl*. Three hours later we are marveling about how Ben Affleck is the movie star you'd most want to plan your bachelor party, and how you didn't really get to see that much of his penis in the shower scene, and we have completely forgotten about our argument. The truth is, the reason I take B.J.'s criticism so hard is that I just want to impress him.

And, of course, he is very difficult to impress. He has impossibly high standards, and you can never predict what he is going to like. For instance, he dislikes the theatre. *All* theatre. Categorically. As a mode of artistic expression.

One time, ten years ago, I got tickets to see the Broadway play *Doubt*. It had won a Tony Award and a Pulitzer Prize, which are my two favorite prizes because they are classy and New Yorky and less thirsty than other awards. I love seeing Broadway shows, because I get to dress up in fancy clothes, but unlike when I attend Hollywood stuff, I get to feel educated and smart while I'm doing it. I feel like a real patron of the arts when I'm flipping through a playbill. "Oooh, what else has this fight choreographer worked on? *Peter Pan*!? I *thought* I recognized that sword play!" I also like that every seventy minutes they give you a break to go drink alcohol and eat candy. But I didn't have anyone to go with, so I begged B.J. to come with me. I could tell he really didn't want to go, but he also didn't have any other plans, and I think *Doubt*'s flashy awards and my second-row orchestra seats swayed him. Also, I lied and said, "I hear it's really fun." I had a fantasy that when the play ended, B.J. would turn to me, emotional, and say: "This experience has completely changed the way I think about theatre. You were right, Min. You are always right. Culturally, you blow me away. Now, what can I buy you to thank you?"

I was careful not to tell B.J. too much about the play beforehand, because *Doubt* is not the most fun play. In fact, I might venture to say it's the *least* fun play. Here's what *Doubt* is about: child abuse at a parochial school, and the cast is two nuns and a priest. As the lights were dimming, I could see B.J. reading the program, realizing with horror that this was not a fun musicalization of a hit comedy movie. This was a small, depressing play about unspeakable acts; that reeked of class, as theatre should be! And he was trapped.

Doubt is a really good play, so for much of the first act, I was too absorbed to check in on B.J. But about forty minutes in, I started hearing little noises next to me. I turned to look at him, and he was shifting his weight in his seat, drumming his fingers on the armrest between us, and letting out little put-upon sighs. B.J. was bored and he was restless. I am 100 percent certain that he was also looking at his phone during the play, but B.J. disputes this vehemently. I elbowed him. We were so close to the stage that the actors could see us! He was going to distract Cherry Jones with his fidgeting! B.J. finally stopped. An hour or so passed.

Then, during a pivotal scene where the priest is being confronted by a nun about his alleged child abuse (almost certain child abuse, IMO, but it's called *Doubt*, so whatever), I glanced over at B.J. again to see if he was paying attention. He wasn't; he was fast asleep. Worse yet, he had fallen asleep on the shoulder of an older gentleman sitting on the other side of him. If the man was bothered by B.J.'s giant head resting on him, he graciously didn't make a big deal about it, which is crazy because B.J.'s head is like 30 percent of his total body weight. All the older gentleman did was throw me a look like: *I guess this guy is just gonna sleep on me?* I mouthed, *I'm so sorry!* and reached over to wake him up. The man shook his head like *No, don't bother*, perhaps knowing that sleeping B.J. was better than fidgety B.J. We both turned back to the play to watch its dramatic conclusion (spoiler alert: I *think* the priest did it, and I *think* the nun had doubt about it?).

Thankfully, at curtain call, the riotous applause and standing ovation woke B.J. up. He was pink-faced and disoriented, like a man who had been asleep for a year. In the cartoon version of this, he might have leapt out of his seat, saying, *Who dat? Where is I?* looking around, frightened, with a long gray beard. B.J. saw that he had been napping on his seatmate and apologized. The man nodded politely.

As soon as the lights came up, several people rushed toward us. My first thought was that these were fans of *The Office* who wanted to talk to B.J. and me, and I was prepared to take a few photos. Ah, the trials of stardom! I thought as I touched up my makeup. I was wrong. They didn't want to talk to us. They wanted to talk to the older gentleman seated next to us. Because it was Edward Albee. Edward Albee, our greatest living playwright, American treasure, who watched *Doubt* from beginning to end and loved it, all while a bored B. J. Novak slept on him.

Once I was recounting this incident at a party, and B.J. responded:

I don't know why you were embarrassed of *me*. The embarrassment should rest squarely on the shoulders of *theatre itself*. If you put me, a well-educated, curious person, interested in seeing a Broadway show, in a second-row seat at the finest play of the year, and you *still* can't prevent me from falling asleep, then there is a problem with your *medium of communication*.

That's verbatim, because I couldn't believe how self-righteous he was being, so I started to record his rant on my phone. I disagree with him *completely*, but I'm actually impressed by his reasoning and charmed by his outrage. He's who I want Donald Trump to be.

I have a feeling B.J. will not like me telling that anecdote, so I want to move on to something he might like a little more.

On the Friday night before Thanksgiving in 2007, B.J. and I were flying from Burbank to New York on a JetBlue red-eye. The flight was packed and there was a celebratory feeling in the air; everyone was flying to the East Coast for a week of vacation. I was drinking a glass of red wine, something I rarely do in life, but it was free and seemed like a cool and decadent thing for a worldly adult to do on a plane. B.J. and I watched *Lost* on his portable DVD player, which is just about the most 2007 thing you can do. Every few minutes I would pause it so he could explain what was going on. About twenty minutes into the flight, the plane began to shake. The captain came on and told us not to worry, that it was just run-of-the-mill turbulence, but then told the flight attendants to take their seats, and we heard the familiar ding of the "seat belts on" sign. If anything, this only enhanced the spooky/suspenseful experience of watching *Lost*.

A minute later, however, the turbulence got worse, way worse, and our TV screens went black. B.J. and I glanced at each other. This is weird. Then the plane seemed to drop thousands of feet in a free fall and then rise up quickly. Then it kept doing that, arbitrarily. Without TVs to distract us, the panic filled the cabin. Our pilot spoke to us again, but gone was the relaxed man who had cooed, "Folks, this is your captain speaking . . ." and made me feel like a valued member of the JetBlue community. "There seems to be some kind of an electrical storm . . . ?" he began, nervously trailing off in a way where the end of his sentence can only be: ". . . which is scaring the shit out of me." Then he says: "This really came out of nowhere. Very weird."

Very weird? You don't get to confide in *us* about what you think is weird, guy! You're supposed to roll with it and tell us everything's fine while you silently sweat it out in the cockpit, rubbing your rosary beads. The uncertainty of our pilot, combined with the random lurching of the plane, caused yet another spike of fear in the passengers. Babies began to cry. Water bottles started rolling down the aisle. I turned back to see the flight attendant seated with her arms folded tightly across her chest. Her eyes were squeezed shut and she was mouthing something. It became clear to me she was praying. If you have never seen a flight attendant praying, I hope you never do, because it is one the scariest things in the whole world. Scarier than when my doctor looks into my ear and gasps. Scarier than that plane crash in *Lost*. Ah! There is a plane crash in *Lost* and now we are going to die in a plane crash while watching *Lost*! And I'm too scared to tell anyone my cool observation!

People had started shouting a bit now, but I was, surprisingly, not one of them. I'm the kind of person who becomes silent when I get scared, because I hope Death will not notice me if I am very still and very quiet. It has worked well so far. And then, after a few minutes, something weird happened. There was a certain inevitability that made me actually *relax*. If this plane was going down, there was nothing I could do. It wasn't like we were trapped in a burning building where I could decide if I should jump out the window or make a rope out of all my clothes and climb down naked. (The answer is rope of clothes, by the way. I have thought about this a lot.) There was nothing to do on a plane but close my eyes, sit, and pretend this was just an amusement-park ride, not a real-life plane that was possibly hurtling us toward our deaths. And if I died, at least I wouldn't have to figure out how to get this red wine stain out of my shirt.

I felt a pain in my arm and looked down to see B.J.'s hands gripping my forearm incredibly tightly. Oh yes, B.J. was here. I had momentarily forgotten him, preoccupied as I was with my death scenarios and my meta *Lost* thoughts. And then I saw something legitimately surprising: There was genuine terror in his huge blue eyes, something I had never seen before.

For anyone who has ever met B.J., the first thing you notice about him is how calm he is. Actually, the first thing you notice is how much he is on his phone. Like more than a tween girl in a fight with her boyfriend. The *second* thing you notice is how calm he is. He has a detached air that makes you think, Whoa, what is that guy *thinking*? and, Boy, *that* guy gets it. He's the kind of person who knows the coolest new place to have dinner and the best new songs on the radio. He knows the most interesting facts about famous people like Steve Wynn, Mark Twain, and Mia Farrow, and can insert them into conversations without seeming like he just looked them up on Wikipedia. It always seems like he's read the entire *New Yorker*, not just the cartoons and those ads for Adirondack chairs. His first impression is the opposite of mine. He's cool and a little elusive. On the other hand, when you meet me, within the first ten minutes I have loudly explained my whole deal to you. With the exception of an auctioneer and maybe Kris Jenner, there is no one in the world less mysterious than me.

And he is so funny. When I first moved to Los Angeles, and I was lonely and homesick for New York, B.J. cheered me up simply by making me laugh. Sometimes it was inadvertent. If you went into the writers' kitchen after B.J. had been there, you could always tell. Several of the cabinet doors would be wide open, and one time he even left the refrigerator door open. It was like a teenage ghost had been there before you and had taken all the Chex Mix and soy milk with him. It was so funny to me. But more often, though, it was intentional. He wrote my favorite joke of all time: "I learned nothing in college. It was really kind of my own fault. I had a double major: psychology and reverse psychology." His impression of the character Stanley Hudson on *The Office* makes me laugh harder than anything. If you ever run into him—even if he's at dinner or on a hike—definitely stop him and have him do his "Stanley." He'll really appreciate you asked, I promise.

I, in return, decided he was the best person I had ever met. In my relationship with B.J., he has always been the more worldly, cleverer, and more poised one. Why? Because he has lived in L.A. longer, he was a comedy writer before me, he is more well read than me, he even seems to understand *Lost* somehow. He has always played that role. Suddenly for the first time ever, he was looking to *me* for reassurance. It felt so foreign to me. "It's going to be OK," I said, not sure if I had ever uttered that phrase to another person. "I promise." He closed his eyes and nodded, his grip on me still tight.

When the plane stabilized a few minutes later, and our pilot reverted to his confident, folksy self—"In a few hours there'll be a great view of the Finger Lakes to your left!"—I felt B.J. relax, and he loosened his grip on my arm. I knew he was a little self-conscious now, but I was happy. When the pilot explained we had to make an emergency stop in Buffalo for more fuel, I nodded at a worried B.J. and said, "It's fine. Don't worry." He was relieved. Most people who know B.J. will go the entire length of their relationship with him without having the moment where he is vulnerably looking to them for help. Now I had experienced it, and I felt closer to him. All it had taken was a dangerous electrical storm that terrorized a plane full of innocent people and ruined one perfectly good shirt with a red wine stain. I think it was worth it.

My mother passed away in 2011. She was a warm and sociable person, but she did not suffer fools. In fact, that policy extended beyond fools. She did not suffer lazy people, pretentious people, liars, the sloppy, or the inarticulate. Basically she suffered very few people, and it was hard to earn her respect. But she always really respected B.J. Maybe it was something about his confidence, but I think it had more to do with the fact that he, like her, is a very serious person who loves nothing more than a smart joke. They had a fondness and mutual respect for each other, even through the tumultuousness of our twenties.

She said of him, "B.J. is your equal," which is saying a lot, because my mother thought I was literally the best person she had ever met.

Later, when she got sick, B.J. came to Boston to visit her in the hospital, and he did something I will always be profoundly grateful for. He did for her what he had done for me when I was a nervous, homesick, heartbroken New York transplant hired on my first writing job on season 1 of *The Office*. He made her laugh.

And that is why B.J. and I are soul mates, and the reason is . . . because in terms of the soul, we like to . . . That doesn't make any sense. We're soup snakes. B.J. and I are soup snakes.

ONE OF THE PRESIDENT'S MEN

I AM AT DINNER WITH A TALL, HANDSOME blond man and I have told myself I will not sleep with him. We are eating at a small-plates restaurant because, in Los Angeles, you are legally required to go to a small-plates restaurant on your third date. I'm a little drunk because I really like the blond man, whose name is Will, and I want him to think I have a carefree personality, which is a lie. I have a very anxious, argumentative personality. Two Moscow Mules become three. I feel myself descending into drunken agreeableness. My outrage about normally hot-button topics fades. "Good for those *Entourage* guys for making a movie!" I hear myself saying. "I can't wait to see what they've been cookin' up all these years!" I am now a textbook great date. Thanks, alcohol!

At the end of the date, I excuse myself to go to the bathroom. The back of my Alexander Wang dress is soaked through with nervous sweat, like I am testifying in front of Judge Judy and I definitely stole my ex-husband's favorite dog. I'm so relieved that I decided to wear black for what feels like the first time in my life. I pat my forehead with a damp paper towel, look in the mirror, and say, "You are a strong, powerful woman with incredible self-discipline." In the low glow of the bathroom light I seem resolute and kind of hot, actually, in an Olivia-Pope-being-tortured-for-state-secrets sort of way. I am so proud.

When I get back to the table, Will has already paid the check and stands as I approach. "Let's go for a walk," he says, matter-of-factly, resting his hand firmly on the small of my back. If he feels how damp my dress is, he doesn't seem to care. "I want to see your place."

Oh my God, I thought. I think I might be about to hook up with someone who works for the president of the United States.

THE LEADER OF THE FREE WORLD
WOULD LIKE TO MEET YOU

May, a Year Earlier

I've attended some pretty glamorous events over the years, like the Costume Ball at the Met, the Golden Globes, and the *Vanity Fair* Oscar party. They are usually held at distinguished cultural institutions like the Met or the Annenberg Center—always beautiful spaces that are home to priceless works of art.

The first thing they do when a Hollywood party rents out the place is push all the art to the corner so it doesn't get in the way. They have to do that so there's room for a red carpet, a bar, a prime rib carving station, a photo booth, and, for some reason, an Acura parked inside, in the middle of the party floor. There's *always* a parked Acura at every major Hollywood party. Who wants to see some boring Winslow Homer when Scarlett Johansson could be getting sliced prime rib while catching a glimpse of a brand-new Acura coupe?

I'm sorry to say that these parties are actually a little bit of a letdown. First of all, the lighting is usually so dim you can't see anything, so you wonder why you even wore your expensive heels that are making your feet bleed when your gardening Crocs would've been more than fine. But the main reason the parties are a letdown is that I have this Cinderella idea that after spending hours getting ready, *something is going to happen at the ball!* But then, when you end up going to the ball, the best thing that happens is, say, you get a gift bag with some Lara Bars in it.

But one year, I became a somewhat frequent guest of the president of the United States, and it *was* like Cinderella.

Several springs ago, I went to New York for the Upfronts, where everyone in television gathers to hobnob with advertisers. The advertisers are usually clean-cut, skittish, fairly indistinguishable executives named Patricia or John. They had all been drinking since nine a.m. on the networks' dime and were completely plastered. Patricia was emboldened to confess to me that she had never seen my show, but would I mind taking a photo with her because it would make her sister so jealous. I teach Patricia how to use the camera on her phone, she and I pose as Charlie's Angels, and when she leaves she kisses me on the lips. That's pretty much what I did for four hours, and it was actually kind of fun.

In the midst of all this, my publicist Alex texted me. She had received a call from a woman named Sarah Fisher, who worked for the president.

"The president of what?" I asked warily, immediately assuming it was the head of a tampon company who wanted me to Instagram a photo of me holding their goods during National Women's Menstruation Week or something.

Alex texted back immediately: "Of the United States." I almost dropped my phone. I excused myself from the Patricias and Johns and went to a quiet corner to call her.

She explained that Sarah Fisher was a huge fan of my book and my show, and, through Instagram, had seen that I was in New York. She was also in New York, traveling with the president for a fund-raiser at the Waldorf Astoria. Later, I would realize that Sarah was one of a small handful of people in President Obama's inner circle and one of the most powerful people in DC. Sarah was calling to see if I would like to come by between events and "spend some time with the president."

Spend some time with the president? Uh, sure, whatever that means! Was I to be presented to the president as a human sex gift, like Marilyn Monroe? I would do that! Would I be able to go to my hotel and change out of my high-waisted comfort briefs first? As I was fantasizing about my life as mistress to the president, I suddenly imagined Michelle Obama's tall, perfectly proportioned body and thought, OK, that's definitely not happening. Never picture First Lady Michelle Obama. She is the death of any presidential romance fantasy you might have.

"Yes! When does he want to see me?" I asked.

"Right now."

Within ninety minutes, I found myself standing outside the Waldorf Astoria. The Waldorf—or "The 'Dorf," which only I call it (and which I am hoping will take off, so please use it)—is an enormous old hotel in midtown Manhattan that is fancy in the way your great-aunt might like; that is to say, it looks exactly like the inside of the *Titanic*. I breezed in, wearing a bright-blue dress I'd been wearing for my press events. It wasn't exactly right, but all of my other outfits were too "Mindy Kaling"—that is, best suited for a New Year's Eve party sponsored by a men's deodorant body spray.

I was somehow expecting that I would be escorted directly to the president, who would appoint me diplomat to some cool little country like French Zaire (I'm assuming that's a place). Instead, I was stopped in the Waldorf lobby by a tall blond man in glasses. He introduced himself as Will and shook my hand firmly. Will had the pleasing, mild accent of someone who is not from New England or New York and was good-looking in a Methodist minister kind of way. After spending ten years in Los Angeles, where all the white people are Jewish, Will was actually exotic to me. He was also wearing a suit, which I rarely see on a man under forty years old. In my line of work, every man wears exactly one outfit: khakis, a *Late Night with Jimmy Fallon* T-shirt, and a hooded sweatshirt. If you don't wear that, people think you are a Scientologist and no one will eat lunch with you.

Will made small talk with me in the elevator. He said he was from Tennessee. "Oh, like the song," I said. He didn't respond. After a beat, I added, "Now, *that's* a song I haven't heard in a while." Another beat. "Great song, though," I concluded.

It was the kind of babbling one does when they are at the first stages of a nervous crush. Oh, God. Do I have a nervous crush on this guy? I thought.

My perception of people in the White House has been shaped 100 percent by Aaron Sorkin. *The West Wing* and *The American President* were to blame for my feelings for this stranger. The idealism and adorability of Rob Lowe and Bradley Whitford had made me long for a civic-minded beau who is constantly making long, important speeches and taking principled stands. As a person who has to be enticed to vote by a sticker that says I VOTED, I'm drawn to people who have strong convictions, and not just about who's the best *Shark Tank* shark. Here was Will, focused and quiet, probably full of eloquent monologues I just hadn't heard yet. This, by the way, is the anatomy of a Mindy Kaling crush. Just bear a passing resemblance to a fictional romantic trope I like and I will love you forever. We're all just trying to find the Mark Darcy of our workplace, aren't we?

After babbling amiably with a silent Will, I followed him to an empty ballroom and he told me to have a seat. I noticed with horror that my phone was dead and, in a desperate tone used only by women begging for their child's life, asked Will if he had a charger.

How would I get a picture with the president with a dead phone? He politely said no and left. I waited there alone for forty-five minutes, growing increasingly nervous. Just when I thought I might sneak out to a bodega and buy a disposable camera, Will came back to check on me. He gave me a bottle of water and thanked me for being so patient. He also pulled a phone charger out of his pocket and handed it to me like contraband. I was so excited that I gave him a hug.

WILL: I had no idea this would make you so happy.
ME: It's just that I was in the middle of a really important game of Candy Crush.

Will chuckled. *A chuckle!* He doesn't hate me! And that's historically all the encouragement I need! I saw my opening.

ME: You're really helpful and nice. I bet you were like, class president.
WILL: Actually, I was. All four years of high school.
ME: This is cool. I'm meeting a lot of presidents today.

As Will was trying to get a handle on my B+ flirting, he got word that I would meet the president. That was a moment when I realized how cool my life is. I was trying to hit on a guy and was being interrupted by the president of the United States. We walked down a hallway, and President Obama emerged from a massive ballroom with Sarah, the woman who had arranged our meeting.

President Obama shook my hand and said, "I hear you like romantic comedies, like my wife."

I almost fainted.

We spoke about movies and storytelling, and then he asked about my parents. I'm one of those people who is infatuated with her parents, so it was thrilling to talk about my mother with him and see him listen intently while I described their journey to this country. But mostly I just beamed at him and let him talk, because I knew this would be a story I tell my grandchildren. Who cares what I said? I forget some of the details of what we talked about, but I will never forget the feeling of being in his presence.

The official White House photographer took a photo of the two of us (didn't need a disposable camera after all!) and Will escorted me back to the lobby of the Waldorf. We rode the elevator in happy silence.

"I could tell he liked you," Will said. I deflected this comment, which is my habit upon receiving any kind of compliment. Will interrupted me and touched my arm. "No, stop. He did."

There are times when I feel especially lucky that I have dark skin, because you can't see me blush. This was one of those times. After Will walked me back to the lobby, I thanked him for the experience and told him to "email me anytime, for anything." He smiled, and not a tight-lipped one either. He said he would, and I believed him.

RE-CON

June

The single best thing about working in a writers' room is that you can disrupt the entire writing process to discuss and investigate your latest crush. My staff on *The Mindy Project* is composed of nine people in their twenties and thirties who have traded the prime of their adulthood for writing jokes on a show about a woman who believes "recycling makes America look poor." And as their leader, I have learned one thing: their hard work must be rewarded with soul-replenishing gossip.

The hardest part of investigating a crush online was that I had deleted my Facebook account five years earlier when I had smartly realized that Facebook would mean an end to my productivity or ever putting on pants. Why go out when I could see pictures from my ex-boyfriend's ex-girlfriend's family trip to Napa? So I did what any reasonable person would do: I made all of the other writers log in to their Facebook accounts to see if they could find Will. We quickly found him but saw that his account was set to private.

We were outraged. "Who the hell does this guy think he is? Harry Connick Jr.?!" we shouted. And then, like Katniss volunteering to be a tribute for her useless sister, Prim, one brave writer, Tracey Wigfield, said she would request Will's friendship on Facebook so we could learn more about him while protecting my identity. I was moved beyond words, which might provide you a glimpse of how truly shallow I am.

Showrunner Matt Warburton asked, "Won't he just look at where she works and figure out pretty easily that she's friends with you?"

"Shut up, Matt!" I barked. *I don't need no logic! I have a crush!*

Of course, Will didn't accept Tracey's friend request because he had no idea who she was.

And then, a month after I met him, out of the blue, Will emailed me. He said the president had enjoyed spending time with me, and asked for an address to send the photo of us. I replied a day later (to show that I was busy, which I was, but not busy enough to not reply immediately), and this kicked off an exchange that lasted more than a year.

Over email I learned that Will traveled everywhere with the president. I also learned that he was very funny, in a dry way. I have the opposite of a dry sense of humor, so I'm always impressed by it. My sense of humor is wet and loud and risqué, like topless day at the water park.

I have a terrible habit of impulsively sending text messages that reveal my true feelings and frighten people off, such as: "I like you so much it scares me." So Jeremy Bronson, one of my closest friends, proofread my communication with Will. Jeremy has been doing that as long as I have been friends with him, so much so that if you ever text with me, there is a 70 percent chance you are actually texting with Jeremy.

Will and I developed a steady texting relationship, but he was always off solving problems for the president. He was one of the few guys I've met who is busier than I am. It was at once frustrating and totally sexy. One day I confessed that I'd had Tracey request his Facebook friendship. This charmed him, and the next day, Tracey raced into the writers' room, excitedly announcing that Will had accepted her friend request. This unlocked a treasure trove of Will-related tidbits, like what city he was born in, that he loved *The Daily Show* and hiking and had gone to the University of Pennsylvania. Even though it was fairly generic and painted a picture of several hundreds of guys we knew, it felt like the most exciting day of my life.

THE STATE DINNER

February

Over the next six months, I discovered another benefit of my new friendship with Will: I began to receive invitations to incredible events in Washington, DC. I was invited to the White House Holiday Party, a luncheon for Asian American artists (I was excited to technically qualify as one), and the White House Easter Egg Roll to read stories to children (excited to be considered a person who doesn't scare children). I could never attend anything because I was filming my show, but I paraded my invitations around the set so people could touch the fancy stationery.

And then one magical day, nine months after our meeting at the

Waldorf, I got an email from the White House saying, in gorgeous presidential cursive: "The President of the United States invites you to a State Dinner honoring François Hollande, the President of France."

It was a save the date for a *state dinner*!

I scrolled to the very unsexy second page, which instructed me, at my earliest convenience, to please provide this long list of incredibly personal information, including my social security number, federal tax identification number, driver's license, and place of birth. It occurred to me that this might be the smartest identity-theft scam ever. But even if it was, I didn't care, because what a glamorous scam! Like the Hollywood Film Awards!

The best part was that Will offered to give me a tour of the White House. I remember bursting into the writers' room and telling everyone. They were excited about the state dinner, but their interest in Will had waned. Like with any good story, they needed a plot twist. Executive producer Charlie Grandy shrugged and said, "Please sleep with him or something before you come back. This story needs to move forward." I nodded, understanding that I had a lot to do in DC.

My trip got off to a rocky start. My flight was delayed and I missed Will's private tour of the White House. How was I going to have a sexy trip if I couldn't even show up for things?!

My guest to dinner was my best friend, Jocelyn, who had taken the train down from New York. We forewent seeing any DC museums or national monuments to order cheeseburgers and watch *Will & Grace* in bed at our hotel, because we are real best friends, not lame fake friends trying to impress each other with how fascinated we are with culture and learning.

I'd hired a hair and makeup team to get us ready. They regularly did hair and makeup for a very famous African American actress, whom I'm dying to tell you about but I can't. (How about this: if you ever run into me on the street I will tell you.) The whole time we were getting ready I was trying to get dirt on this actress but they revealed nothing, which drove me crazy, because celebrity secrets are more valuable than diamonds. The only thing I was able to sneak out of them was that the actress uses Preparation H on her face as a primer before makeup. I loved this so much that I insisted they do the same to me.

I have Preparation H smeared all over my face in these pictures. I have no idea what it does to the sphincter, but it keeps my makeup looking flawless.

As you are ushered to the receiving line to meet the president and First Lady, they announce you, *My Fair Lady*–style: "The Honorable

So and So and his wife, Madeline." Just before our turn, the aide asked me how I would describe Jocelyn's and my relationship, and, of course, I prattled on about our backstory as if he were a therapist, not knowing he wanted a succinct answer. So our formal announcement was literally "Miss Mindy Kaling and her best friend from Dartmouth College, Miss Jocelyn Leavitt."

I didn't have time to feel too embarrassed, though, because all of a sudden we were talking to the Obamas. Here is the part of the story where I feel really cool. Instead of shaking my hand, as he was doing with everyone else on the receiving line, the president heard my name, lit up, and hugged me. He then said to his wife, "This is Mindy. Malia was reading her book in Hawaii." *My* book! Malia Obama was reading *my* book! The one Amazon.com reviewer "My2Cents" called "sort of meh"! I was walking on air.

And then I saw Will.

Will stood next to and slightly behind the First Lady, dutiful and handsome in his dark suit. I was still beaming from my interaction with the Obamas, so when I saw him, I called out "Will!" and pulled him into a tight hug. From the way he reacted, I got the distinct feeling that you are not supposed to embrace the man standing to the right of the First Lady, but I didn't care. He looked great, he smelled great, and I looked great, and smelled like my hotel's tiny complimentary body lotion. So I impulsively topped the hug with a kiss on the cheek.

"I'm so sorry I missed the tour!" I said, very loudly, surprised how important it was to me that he know.

"Me too," he answered, making such textbook-good eye contact that the hairs on my arm stood up.

For a moment we said nothing, just two wordless idiots smiling at each other, with the most important people in the world standing a foot away. The First Lady, now on to greeting the people next in line, glanced over at us with a curious look on her face. I realized it was time to leave, so I uttered my classic Mindy Kaling parting line: "Well, this was cool!" and Jocelyn thankfully pulled me away. I wonder if it was the First Lady who told Will he had lipstick on his cheek.

Jocelyn and I were shuttled by trolley to the dinner, the equivalent of the most beautiful tented wedding you have ever seen, set up in the shadow of the White House.

Stephen Colbert and his wife were seated in front of us on the shuttle. I tried to work up the courage to say hello to him, but I was too nervous, so I just gazed at the back of his head. I was so close I could've stroked it, lovingly. Should I have done it? It's a close call.

(I should mention that Stephen was not only seated at the president's table for dinner but was actually sitting on the other side of the First Lady herself. A year later, when I was a guest on *The Colbert Report*, I brought this up to Stephen shyly, backstage. He told me that before that dinner, he didn't even know them. So, the president and First Lady just wanted to sit next to Stephen Colbert because, well, he's Stephen fucking Colbert. Way to be, guy.)

The state dinner looked and felt as luxe and fancy as an *SNL* parody of a state dinner. It's nuts. If you think about it, it is one of the only government-sponsored events where the décor and food are supposed to be so extravagant that the invited foreign head of state goes home and says, "Guys, you will not *believe* how they do dinners in America." The salads were served in delicate glass horticulture bowls. The butter was molded into the shape of a tiny, intricate bow. It was not one of my usual Hollywood events, like *GalStyle Weekly*'s "Hot Gays Under Thirty" Awards. This was historic. This was the kind of place a girl could leave her glass slipper with the reasonable hope that a prince might track her down. Or, in my case, my Jimmy Choo size 39s with orthotic inserts.

We got drunk. The kind of drunk where you are eating off the dessert plate of someone very high up at the NSA and you're not even worried they're going to wiretap your email later.

I saw John Kerry talking to Bradley Cooper. I'm from Massachusetts and I'm friends with Ed Helms, so I figured I had hit the conversational jackpot with these two. I was drunk and feeling a little important, so I wandered over and interrupted them. "Hi! I'm Mindy Kaling. I'm from Massachusetts. Ed Helms was in *The Hangover* and was also on my old show, *The Office*," I said cockily. By this time next year, John, Bradley, and I would be sipping hot cocoa in Teresa Heinz's Idaho ski chalet. "So, we have him in common."

"Yes," Bradley responded. "I know Ed."

I would give our interaction a solid B-minus.

Bradley Cooper later revealed on *The View* that he was not wearing underwear
that night. Doesn't that make this not-great photo a little sexier?

I sat back down next to Jocelyn, and Mary J. Blige began her
performance. My drunken bravery streak continued, and I texted
Will.

> ME: Where are you? Mary J. Blige is singing. Elena Kagan looks
> hot as hell. *How are you missing this?*

He responded sweetly that he wished he was there and hoped I
was having fun.

Having fun? WTF? Is he my aunt? Hours later, back at our hotel,
Jocelyn and I dissected every detail of his texts. Had I been imag-
ining that he was into me? Was my fondness for him completely
one-sided? I felt foolish, like when I was eleven years old and wrote
to Christian Slater's agent telling him how much I loved him and
would he let me be his intern-slash-girlfriend when I went to high
school in three years? I never got a response.

I got texts from the writers asking what happened. "We're

engaged!" I wrote back. Then, quickly, "No we're not. That was a sad joke. Nothing happened. Go back to work."

WHITE HOUSE CORRESPONDENTS DINNER

April

A few months later, *The New Yorker* invited me to be a guest at their table at the White House Correspondents Dinner. I didn't bother telling Will I was going, because, well, I had done that before. We were just friendly, platonic acquaintances, like me and Chelsea Handler.

But Will found out and texted me. He asked if he could finally take me on that tour of the White House and West Wing. I said yes.

It's funny when you decide you don't like someone. I am the kind of person who, if my feelings are unrequited, can completely detach from someone emotionally if I simply put my mind to it. That's why I'm always saying I would be a great serial murderer.

That's what I did with Will. It was like flipping a light switch. He was no longer a Washington, DC, crush on whom I had pinned my whimsical hopes and dreams. He was a pleasant and civic-minded tour guide from Tennessee. He didn't seem as tall to me anymore. His accent was more unsophisticated than adorable. I could look at him and go "Meh."

The tour was lovely and, to be honest, I was happy I was actually paying attention to it rather than to Will. The Oval Office, the Navy Mess Hall, those are all historic places that deserve not to be sullied by romantic motives. As I was leaving, he told me to text him after the dinner. I said I would, but I knew I wouldn't. Light switch.

Attending the Correspondents Dinner as a guest of *The New*

Yorker was a dream realized, especially since none of the editors touched any of the rolls in our artisanal bread basket, which meant I could have at 'em. While I chewed on my eleven brioche rolls, I saw the likes of Gen. David Petraeus, Sen. Kirsten Gillibrand, and that guy from *Magic Mike*, who also played a hot werewolf and was supposed to have a huge wang. It was an extremely glamorous night.

Just before two a.m. I got a text from Will asking if I wanted to "meet him for a drink." We all know what two a.m. drinks mean. If I'm texting Chelsea Handler at two a.m., friendly acquaintance is going right out the window.

I didn't respond and left for L.A. that morning.

MY WEIRD NEW MALE FRIEND

May

Will came to L.A. in the spring for a week and wanted to see me. I no longer considered him a romantic option, but he was a well-connected DC person who could maybe make it so I didn't have to pay my taxes. We ended up meeting at a bar the writers frequent, and ran into Jeremy and Matt, who joined us for a drink. That was such a great coincidence, because until that moment, I think they thought it was plausible I had made Will up. After that bar, Will and I headed to another bar. It was fun but it didn't exactly feel like a date, and that was OK.

But then something happened and suddenly it did feel like a date, in a big way. We slipped into a cab to meet some of his friends at a dive bar across town. When the cab pulled away from the curb, he turned to me and said, "Put your seat belt on."

"What? We're in the backseat," I replied. I never wear a seat belt in the backseat; I barely like doing it when I'm driving because it presses on my boobs funny. Instead of responding, Will slowly reached over, his face inches from mine, pulled my seat belt across me, his fingers grazing my body, and buckled it, completely serious. "It's not safe," he whispered. I could feel his warm breath on my face. I wanted him to kiss me so badly. At the next bar, I think I met his friends, I might have talked to them, I don't really remember. All I thought about was him saying, "It's not safe" as he put my seat belt on for me.

Then he dropped me off in a cab and we said goodbye in the car. No kiss, just a hug. A heartfelt hug coming from a straight man who has spent the evening drinking with you is like him buying a billboard in Times Square that says I AM NOT ATTRACTED TO YOU. I walked into my house, got into bed with all my clothes on, and cried.

At work the next day, people were excited. "Jeremy and Matt say Will exists!" they said, wanting to know details of our night together.

"He's not interested. I think I just have a weird new male friend," I announced to them, explaining my night. They booed.

And at that moment, I got a text. It was Will, on *Air Force One*, about to take off back to Washington:

I should've kissed you. That's on me.

I stared at my phone, so angry I almost threw it across the room. This guy was driving me insane. What did I do to deserve this? I was just a friendly thirty-four-year-old TV actress looking for a boyfriend who didn't have a neck tattoo. OK, fine, at this point he could even have a couple of Grateful Dead bears marching across his neck and I'd deal with it. What I didn't need was some hot-and-cold long-distance flake wasting my time. It hurt my feelings and made me feel like something was wrong with me. I deleted all our texts and emails and didn't respond further to any communication from him.

Then, more than a month later, on my birthday, a package arrived for me from Washington. It was a present from Will: a large box filled with treats he had selected especially for me. There was a comedy book by the comedian Don Novello, whom we had talked about on one of our dates; a huge box of chocolate-covered fruit from his favorite chocolatier in Seattle; amazing photos of the president, the First Lady, and me; and a handwritten note on White House stationery describing why he selected all the gifts and wishing me happy birthday. It was one of the more romantic gifts I've ever gotten.

My writing staff ate the chocolates in puzzled silence, none of us knowing what to make of this gesture. My assistant, Sonia, broke the silence by saying, "I think this is what they call mixed signals." Sonia was right. This was 100 percent authentic, real mixed fuckin' signals.

BACK FOR MORE

July, where this story started

Will (now renamed "Trouble Don't Pick Up" in my phone) came to L.A. with the president and asked me to dinner. I listened to his message but didn't return his call.

But then I kept thinking about him.

Well, maybe I could go, I thought, gazing at "Trouble Don't Pick Up Missed Call."

And then it became: Maybe I *should* go.

Why was I even entertaining this? Well, I don't know why exactly. Maybe because, well, in spite of everything, I was still intrigued by Will. I'm not proud of it, and it's a little embarrassing to write, but sometimes you like the idea of someone so much, you just want to do whatever it takes to make it work. And Will was so much better than the other guys I'd been on dates with. He was smart and accomplished, and he wasn't competitive with me. Most important, he was genuine and his job was honorable. I didn't know a lot of people whose job I could describe as "honorable," and, well, I liked being around someone like that. And, it's worth reminding you that Will was a handsome blond man, and how often do you see an actual adult blond man these days? He was basically a priceless orchid. So yeah, maybe I wanted to give him five or six more chances than the average guy I might date.

So, against my better judgment, I called Trouble Don't Pick Up and said, "Sure."

It had been two months since I had last seen Will. I told myself I wouldn't sleep with him and expected that to be easy. Why shouldn't it? The last time I saw him he had hugged me like my mailwoman Rita does when I give her her Christmas bonus. As it turned out, he was a little more attracted to me than Rita was.

SHAKE IT OFF

So yeah, Will spent the night. The next morning when he was leaving, he was so shy and adorable in my foyer that when he left and I closed the door, I covered my mouth with my hand to muffle my crushed-out squeal.

AHHHHH YOU ARE SO CUTE YOU ARE SO FUCKING CUTE YOU ARE SO CUTE!

I was so into him. Sonia brought me a McDonald's Extra Value Meal #1 (the meal she rewards me with after a late night of writing or, extremely rarely, a late night of passion). I was already concocting Will's and my happy ending, in the way only a woman whose job it is to write romantic comedies can. We'd probably get engaged in a year, he'd become a senator, and I'd move to Washington, giving up my career to become a full-time political trophy wife. I'd learn the chronological order of the presidents and get really smart about the news. Just that slightly crazy, embarrassing stuff you think about the night after you first sleep with someone.

But as you probably guessed, since I am not currently the wife of a senator, it didn't work out that way.

Will and I continued to text and email, and would try to see each other, but it never seemed to crystallize into anything more. Whenever he would visit L.A. with the president, I was shooting the show; whenever I would invite him to a party I was throwing, he was traveling. It felt to me like I was making more of an effort than he was, and when I sensed that, I pulled back, not returning his calls or texts because I felt hurt. But none of that mattered, because I knew the truth, which is if someone really wants to see you, they always find a way. Always. That hurt my heart, but I realized, unlike in past relationships when I was younger, it didn't need to be dramatic. Will and I didn't know each other that well; I couldn't even remember if he had any siblings, or what month his birthday was. I knew I had the power to make this a big deal if I wanted to, but the truth is, I wasn't in my twenties anymore—in a good way! Obviously there's a part of all of us who wants to pull a full Courtney Love about every breakup—it's so dramatic and makes you feel like: *See?! You'll remember me one way or another, dammit!* But spending a lot of time and energy nursing a breakup is just not a good use of my time now. Which is too bad, because if you heard my haunting rendition of "Will You Still Love Me Tomorrow" while I wept in the shower during a breakup, you would be moved as hell.

Sometimes a story just needs an ending, and I used to not be a creative enough person to think of an ending to a romantic story that isn't a wedding or a death. This story didn't end in fireworks, because the truth is, fireworks are something from my twenties. I could have made fireworks, but I chose to make a nuanced memory of a person who is neither a hero nor a villain in my life. All I had to do now was move on. In the words of both Mariah Carey and Taylor Swift, I knew I could shake it off. How could it not be true if *both* songs have the same name?

A PERFECTLY REASONABLE REQUEST

W HAT I'M ASKING FOR IS NOT THAT
much. I just want a boyfriend who is
sweet and trustworthy. That's it.

He doesn't need to have a perfect body or look like George Clooney. I want a guy who wants to curl up on a Friday night and watch
Netflix. He can even pick the show. I mean, ideally, it's serialized
and female-driven, and maybe not that boring political one. But
honestly, I don't care. It's not important.

All I want is someone reasonable who is basically a good guy.
Someone patient, who doesn't mind if I'm taking an extra few
minutes getting ready before we leave the house. But who is impatient with the same things that I am, like when we are waiting
too long to be seated for dinner and he should maybe go talk to the
hostess. Because otherwise, why did we make a reservation at all?

I want a guy who is a feminist, someone who knows that all
that means is that men and women are equal. A man who admires
strong women, like Hillary Clinton or Ruth Bader Ginsburg. But
not that really accomplished woman from his office who seems
cool and put-together. I don't mean her. I'd like him to resent her

irrationally, actually. I mean older, strong women in the theoretical.

And I don't need some über-rich hedgefunder either. He just needs to be successful enough to financially support himself. And me and our children if I take time off from work after the babies are born. I just want him to love his job; I don't care about how much money he makes. Just as long as it pays enough to give me the option to go back to work part-time if I decide to pursue my hobby professionally, which is photographing cool manicures for Instagram.

I'm not even one of those women who doesn't want their boyfriend to watch porn. I think it's hot! As long as I'm watching it with him, and there's some kind of entry point for women, like *Fifty Shades of Grey* or *Magic Mike*.

One thing I definitely don't need is lavish gifts. I'm not some princess living in a fairy tale. A simple compliment once in a while is enough to show he appreciates me: "You look pretty today." "I love your laugh." "You're such a good cook, even better than my mother and my sisters." "I love you more than my mother and my sisters." See? It's so easy!

I don't get why that's asking so much, to meet a nice guy at a bar who wants to date for six months and then propose to me while we are in Montana glamping, on a night that is perfectly clear, and then, move out of his apartment, give up his dog to his coworker, and buy a four-bedroom house in the town where I was raised, near that elementary school everyone's raving about.

That's why I think I should date an older guy. They say older guys are more secure and have gotten all the immaturity out of their systems. That would be so refreshing right now. To be with a man who isn't obsessed with youth and doesn't want to stay out late smoking weed with his loser friends. And I don't care if he has kids. I think that's cool! So as long as his kids are already away at college and his wife is dead, I'm in. And she needs to be normal dead, where she won't come back to haunt me as a ghost.

'Cause that's all I want. A sweet, mature, normal, loving guy, with no baggage. And who has an absolutely enormous penis.

A PERFECT COURTSHIP IN MY
ALTERNATE LIFE

I F I HAD STAYED IN NEW YORK AND HAD A non-Hollywood job, I'm certain I would have become a Latin teacher at a private school in Manhattan. I took Latin from seventh grade through college, and I always loved it and was pretty good at it. There weren't a lot of us who took Latin in high school, but our small group felt very cool. Every winter, the Latin Club celebrated Saturnalia, an ancient Roman festival in honor of the deity Saturn. We wore togas (bedsheets unenthusiastically supplied to us by our mothers) and wreaths made out of pipe cleaners, and had a feast of whole roast chickens and carbonated grape juice, which we ate with our hands, like the Romans. We toasted each other by saying "Io Saturnalia!" and pretended to be drunk emperors in the teachers' multipurpose room. You know, just the typical stuff you do when you are really cool in high school.

When I moved to New York after college, I pictured myself teaching Latin at the Dalton School, where Jocelyn worked as a geography teacher. Dalton is on the Upper East Side and felt very glamorous and *Gossip Girl* to me, so I was always coming up with reasons to visit her there. It's a little strange to be in an environment where you are twenty-three and you know the high school students around you are better dressed, more sophisticated, and have had way more sexual experience than you have. They could tell too, I bet, because I was so intimidated I barely made eye contact with any of them. But I'm the kind of person who actually likes feeling a little bit out of place. Aspirational is how I feel comfortable.

The dream of teaching Latin disappeared, of course, when I moved to Los Angeles to work in show business. But I always wondered, in the *Sliding Doors* version of my life, about this other, imaginary version of me, living in New York, teaching at a prep school, and trying to make friends. Over the years, as the real me grew older in L.A., "Mindy in New York" stayed twenty-five. She began to resemble me less and less, and became a character all her own.

I started ascribing fun and theatrical personality traits to her. She partied too much and dated guys in ways that blew up in her face spectacularly, but she still desperately wanted to find love. She was so fun to write that other characters sprung up in her universe. Mindy always fought with one male teacher in particular, a serious-minded forty-year-old US History teacher. I will have a stern man in anything I ever write; I just love a gruff guy with a heart of gold. I guess what I'm saying is Walter Matthau is the man of my dreams.

I thought I would share some of her adventures with you. It's kind of a Choose Your Own Adventure, or Robert Frost's poem "The Road Not Taken," depending on how fancy you are. Enjoy.

MONDAY

From: Mindy Kaling
To: All Faculty
Subject: A Back to School Soiree Chez Mindy
Date: Mon, Sep 5, 2005

Hello, Dalton friends!

Welcome back to another school year. I hope you're all as rested and excited as I am to tackle this new semester. As some of you may know, I was lucky enough to travel to Rome by myself this summer. Traveling by oneself poses its unique challenges, but I think I learned *a lot* and I even brushed up on my Latin. You can read about it in my blog www.aromeofonesown.com. If you do, please let me know what you think by leaving a comment!

I thought it could be fun to have you all over to my new place for drinks. As some of you may know, I no longer live in Gramercy with Ethan, I live in Astoria now. Astoria is a bustling neighborhood with a vibrant culture and, according to a few blogs, Queens is the new Brooklyn. The great part is, I have a lot more space, and not just because I don't have to share it with my ex-boyfriend, ha-ha. But you can decide for yourself! Party info:

This Saturday, Sept 10th @ Chez Mindy
36-19 Ditmars Blvd. Apt. 6A
Astoria
9pm–who knows! :-D
Dress code: *Upscale Autumn*

Anyway, please RSVP if you can make it. I'm really looking forward to seeing you.

Love,
Mindy

Mindy Kaling
Latin Teacher, High School
The Dalton School
108 E 89th St, New York, NY 10128
(212) 555-1445 (work)
(617) 453-8688 (cell)
Tumblr: aromeofonesown.tumblr.com
AIM handle: LatinLover1979
—You can also catch me on Facebook—
"Since you been gone, I can breathe for the first time."
—Kelly Clarkson

From: Sam Cook
To: All Faculty
Subject: RE: A Back to School Soiree Chez Mindy
Date: Mon, Sep 5, 2005

Dear colleagues,

I am actually glad that Ms. Kaling wrote, because it's the beginning of the school year, and we have an opportunity to set a precedent. These email accounts were given to us for work-related emails only, and I would like to keep my inbox clear of irrelevant emails not necessary to education.

SC

Sam Cook
US History, High School
Chair, History Department
The Dalton School
108 E 89th St, New York, NY 10128

From: Mindy Kaling
To: All Faculty
Subject: RE: RE: A Back to School Soiree Chez Mindy
Date: Mon, Sep 5, 2005

Hello everyone,

It has recently been brought to my attention that I may have offended some of you by inviting you to a party on my work email. I am so sorry to have filled your inbox with "irrelevant emails not necessary to education."

It should be noted, however, certain studies have shown that teachers getting along socially actually *benefits* students, so forgive me if I'm trying to do something progressive here. I didn't know this was East Germany in the 1950s where we're not supposed to talk. I'm sure that environment is much worse for the students but I don't have a study to corroborate that. For those who do want to come, please RSVP.

Sorry again if I offended, though I would be *really* surprised if I did.

Mindy Kaling

Mindy Kaling
Latin Teacher, High School
The Dalton School
108 E 89th St, New York, NY 10128
(212) 555-1445 (work)
(617) 453-8688 (cell)
Tumblr: aromeofonesown.tumblr.com
AIM handle: LatinLover1979
—You can also catch me on Facebook—

"Since you been gone, I can breathe for the first time."
—Kelly Clarkson

From: Sam Cook
To: All Faculty
Subject: RE: RE: RE: A Back to School Soiree Chez Mindy
Date: Mon, Sep 5, 2005

Great. Thanks.

SC

Sam Cook
US History, High School
Chair, History Department
The Dalton School
108 E 89th St, New York, NY 10128

TUESDAY

From: Mindy Kaling
To: All Faculty
Subject: Hurtful but work-related matter
Date: Tue, Sep 6, 2005

To all:

You don't have to come to my party, and I get it if you think I
suck and Astoria is lame, but you don't have to talk loudly about
it in the teachers' lounge, where a teacher could walk by on
her break and hear what you are saying, which *is exactly what
happened to me this afternoon.* I know that my party may not
be what you want to do on a Saturday night, and yeah, maybe
it was a mistake to buy a piñata, but I thought it might be a fun
way to blow off steam. The truth is, my apartment is new and
empty and it would have been nice to have it filled with voices.

But you know what? No one has to come. Forget it. Party's canceled.

Sorry to have wasted all your time.
Mindy Kaling

Mindy Kaling
Latin Teacher, High School
The Dalton School
108 E 89th St, New York, NY 10128
(212) 555-1445 (work)
(617) 453-8688 (cell)
Tumblr: aromeofonesown.tumblr.com
AIM handle: LatinLover1979
—You can also catch me on Facebook—

"Since you been gone, I can breathe for the first time."
—Kelly Clarkson

From: Sam Cook
To: Mindy Kaling
Subject: RE: Hurtful but work-related matter
Date: Tue, Sep 6, 2005

Ms. Kaling,

I want to apologize. I was one of the people you overheard talking in the lounge earlier today. I think your party sounds very silly, but I shouldn't have said anything. Please don't cancel it.

And as it happens, I do think piñatas are fun. My daughter Molly really enjoys them, and at her last birthday party, I even took a whack. I think it will go over well.

SC

Sam Cook
US History, High School
Chair, History Department
The Dalton School
108 E 89th St, New York, NY 10128

From: Mindy Kaling
To: Sam Cook
Subject: RE: RE: Hurtful but work-related matter
Date: Tue, Sep 6, 2005

Dear Sam,

Thanks for apologizing, kind of. I do appreciate it, because from someone as disagreeable as you, it must've taken a lot to send that. I forgive you, and I won't cancel the party. You are re-invited.

Though it might not have been apparent in the first email, it's kind of a singles event, so you should come. You and I have that in common at least. Ethan dumped me, and your wife left you. So join us if you're not doing anything.

Sincerely,
Mindy

Mindy Kaling
Latin Teacher, High School
The Dalton School
108 E 89th St, New York, NY 10128
(212) 555-1445 (work)
(617) 453-8688 (cell)
Tumblr: aromeofonesown.tumblr.com
AIM handle: LatinLover1979
—You can also catch me on Facebook—

"Since you been gone, I can breathe for the first time."
—Kelly Clarkson

From: Sam Cook
To: Mindy Kaling
Subject: RE: RE: RE: Hurtful but work-related matter
Date: Tue, Sep 6, 2005

Ms. Kaling,

Thank you for your touching email. I should just clear something up: my wife didn't leave me, she died. Though I am wondering about my behavior in general if you think that the former is more likely.

I don't think I will be able to come to the party.

Sam Cook
US History, High School
Chair, History Department
The Dalton School
108 E 89th St, New York, NY 10128

From: Mindy Kaling
To: Sam Cook
Subject: RE: RE: RE: RE: Hurtful but work-related matter
Date: Tue, Sep 6, 2005

OH MY GOD I am so sorry that I assumed your wife left you.

Sincerely,
Mindy

P.S. I'm also so sorry she is dead.

Mindy Kaling
Latin Teacher, High School
The Dalton School
108 E 89th St, New York, NY 10128
(212) 555-1445 (work)
(617) 453-8688 (cell)
Tumblr: aromeofonesown.tumblr.com
AIM handle: LatinLover1979

—You can also catch me on Facebook—

"Since you been gone, I can breathe for the first time."
—Kelly Clarkson

WEDNESDAY

From: Mindy Kaling
To: Lindsay Kellogg
Subject: hi! And, favor.
Date: Wed, Sep 7, 2005

Hey Linds! I'm so excited you're coming Saturday night! I know how busy you are at Goldmans so I will make sure it's extra fun. Uh, I feel a little embarrassed asking this, but remember that guy Seth you work with? The one you said once looked at our Facebook album from college and said he'd never been with an Indian girl but he'd like to someday? Maybe you could invite him to the party? If it's not weird. It would be really nice to meet some guys.

xoxo

Mindy Kaling
Latin Teacher, High School
The Dalton School
108 E 89th St, New York, NY 10128
(212) 555-1445 (work)
(617) 453-8688 (cell)
Tumblr: aromeofonesown.tumblr.com
AIM handle: LatinLover1979
—You can also catch me on Facebook—

"Since you been gone, I can breathe for the first time."
—Kelly Clarkson

From: Lindsay Kellogg
To: Mindy Kaling
Subject: RE: hi! And, favor.
Date: Wed, Sep 7, 2005

Fuck yeah, I'm coming

This week's BEEN A NIGHTMARE

I've been here like 18 hours/day

Two days ago a partner hung himself

Yikes

I NEED THIS

I'll tell Seth. Should I bring coke?

Linds

Lindsay Kellogg
Vice President, Private Wealth Advisor
Goldman, Sachs & Co.
200 West Street
New York, NY 10282
United States
(212) 902-1000

From: Mindy Kaling
To: Lindsay Kellogg
Subject: RE: RE: hi! And, favor.
Date: Wed, Sep 7, 2005

PLEASE DO NOT BRING COCAINE! It's not going to be that

kind of party, it's mostly high school language arts and history teachers. I got a piñata, which I've heard adults actually like. Promise me you won't bring cocaine.

Mindy Kaling
Latin Teacher, High School
The Dalton School
108 E 89th St, New York, NY 10128
(212) 555-1445 (work)
(617) 453-8688 (cell)
Tumblr: aromeofonesown.tumblr.com
AIM handle: LatinLover1979
—You can also catch me on Facebook—
"Since you been gone, I can breathe for the first time."
—Kelly Clarkson

From: Lindsay Kellogg
To: Mindy Kaling
Subject: RE: RE: RE: hi! And, favor.
Date: Wed, Sep 7, 2005

Yeah ok I won't "bring any coke with me." ;-)

I will bring Seth.

Lindsay Kellogg
Vice President, Private Wealth Advisor
Goldman, Sachs & Co.
200 West Street
New York, NY 10282
United States
(212) 902-1000

This message w/attachments (message) is intended solely for the use of the intended recipient(s) and may contain information that is privileged, confidential or proprietary. If you are not an intended recipient, please notify the sender, and then please delete and destroy all copies and attachments, and be advised that any review or dissemination of, or the taking of any action in reliance on, the information contained in or attached to this message is prohibited.

THURSDAY

From: Mindy Kaling
To: Sam Cook
Subject: Ugh
Date: Thurs, Sep 8, 2005

Dear Sam,

I hope you don't mind me writing, but I was passing by your office and heard Henry Guilford's parents yelling at you, even though the door was closed. I know it sounds like I was eavesdropping but I swear I wasn't!

I just wanted to say that a) it sounded awful b) Henry Guilford is a little shit, and c) they have yelled at me too. Henry wrote an essay sophomore year on Cicero that read like a Columbia undergrad's thesis presentation, which I'm almost certain it was. There's no way a kid whose YouTube channel is videos of him tripping bike messengers and filming it could have written that essay.

Anyway, just because this school has a lot of rich kids I don't think their parents should be able to just scream at us. And if it makes you feel any better, at assembly just last week, I heard some junior girls saying that you were the best history teacher in the department. Wow, I guess I do eavesdrop a lot.

Mindy

P.S. Should you reconsider coming to my party, I think you'll find it a really memorable evening. Plus I'm really worried no one's going to come.

Mindy Kaling
Latin Teacher, High School
The Dalton School
108 E 89th St, New York, NY 10128
(212) 555-1445 (work)

(617) 453-8688 (cell)
Tumblr: aromeofonesown.tumblr.com
AIM handle: LatinLover1979
—You can also catch me on Facebook—
"Ladies leave yo man at home, the club is full of ballas and they pockets full grown." —Destiny's Child

---

From: Sam Cook
To: Mindy Kaling
Subject: RE: Ugh
Date: Thurs, Sep 8, 2005

Mindy,

I'm sorry you heard that. In the middle of Carol Guilford's screaming at me about my grading system, my mind began to wander. I took this teaching job all those years ago so I could spend the summers writing a novel, but I've written nothing, and yet I still have this job.

You wouldn't want me at your party, I'm fifteen years older than virtually everyone else attending. I also could not begin to understand what the dress code "Upscale Autumn" means.

Thank you for your kind note.

Sam

Sam Cook
US History, High School
Chair, History Department
The Dalton School
108 E 89th St, New York, NY 10128

From: Mindy Kaling
To: Sam Cook
Subject: RE: RE: Ugh
Date: Thurs, Sep 8, 2005

You're writing a novel? I've never even *read* a novel. I guess that's not true, I've read *Bridget Jones's Diary* and the sequel, but besides that, not much. I know, v. depressing. Don't worry about the dress code, I only did that for Madame Burkholtz and the rest of the French Department. You would think people who specialize in Romance languages would dress better! I think you dress nicely, though I've never really thought about it. You look like a presidential candidate during the Depression.

I better go finish burning CDs for the party. See ya!

MK

From: Mindy Kaling
To: Jim Dufault
Subject: Hello
Date: Fri, Sep 9, 2005

Dear Big Jim,

First, a compliment. The hallways have been looking so clean this year and I see almost no gum jammed in the hinges of any lockers. The custodial staff has a very challenging job and I commend you. Second, a short funny story: I am so used to calling you "Big Jim" that I realized I didn't actually know your last name. Then I found out it was Dufault, which is so beautiful. What is your ancestry?

I was also wondering if I could borrow a couple of the plastic garbage bins, if the janitorial department could spare them. I'd like to use them as drink coolers for a party I'm having this weekend, which you are *of course* invited to. And while I'm asking for things, maybe I could take a few rolls of paper towels. I think there are quite a few of them in the supply closet and I doubt that anyone would miss them here at school.

With utmost respect for what you do,
Mindy Kaling

Mindy Kaling
Latin Teacher, High School
The Dalton School
108 E 89th St, New York, NY 10128
(212) 555-1445 (work)
(617) 453-8688 (cell)
Tumblr: aromeofonesown.tumblr.com
AIM handle: LatinLover1979
—You can also catch me on Facebook—
"Ladies leave yo man at home, the club is full of ballas and they pockets full grown." —Destiny's Child

---

From: Sam Cook
To: Susan Cook-Velazquez
Subject: babysitting?
Date: Fri, Sep 9, 2005

Suze,

By any chance, are you free tomorrow night if I dropped Molly off? She has homework and she says that at ten she "really doesn't need babysitting anymore." I know it's last minute, but a work thing came up.

Your loving brother,
Sam

Sam Cook
US History, High School
Chair, History Department
The Dalton School
108 E 89th St, New York, NY 10128

From: Mindy Kaling
To: Madeleine Resnick-Klein
Subject: Hello
Date: Fri, Sep 9, 2005

Dear Madeleine,

I cannot begin to tell you how upset I am that I was twenty minutes late to our scheduled meeting this afternoon to discuss the National Latin Exam. A headmistress shouldn't have to deal with extreme tardiness from teachers in addition to your other responsibilities.

I'll be honest, a younger version of me would've lied and told you it was because I had subway trouble. But, if I've learned anything from my recent breakup, it's that I only have room for truth in my life. And if I expect it from my lovers, I must be honest with people in my professional life like you. The truth is, I did not have subway trouble, I was at the European Wax Center on 63rd Street getting waxed for a party tomorrow night, and I passed out when they were waxing a sensitive area. When I came to, I realized I was late, raced over to our meeting, and thus we find ourselves in our present situation.

Actually, this is a good opportunity to encourage to you to attend my party. Please come!

Very sorry,
Mindy Kaling

Mindy Kaling
Latin Teacher, High School
The Dalton School
108 E 89th St, New York, NY 10128

(212) 555-1445 (work)
(617) 453-8688 (cell)
Tumblr: aromeofonesown.tumblr.com
AIM handle: LatinLover1979
—You can also catch me on Facebook—
"Ladies leave yo man at home, the club is full of ballas and they pockets full grown." —Destiny's Child

---

From: Madeleine Resnick-Klein
To: Mindy Kaling
Subject: RE: Hello
Date: Fri, Sep 9, 2005

Ms. Kaling,

Your excuse is inappropriate, your email is inappropriate, please never be late again, and change your email signature. I will not be attending your party.

Madeleine

Madeleine Resnick-Klein, PhD
Headmistress
The Dalton School
108 E 89th St, New York, NY 10128

From: Susan Cook-Velazquez
To: Sam Cook
Subject: RE: babysitting?
Date: Fri, Sep 9, 2005

Sure I can take Molls. I'm intrigued about this "Saturday night work event." I think that sounds like a really good thing for you, professionally. ;-)

Can I ask more about it?

XO

From: Lindsay Kellogg
To: Mindy Kaling
Subject: Yo
Date: Fri, Sep 9, 2005

If I'm gonna bring Seth to the party, there better be some single guys there

And not any Teach For America bullshit

Someone legit cute

Dude I need to have sex

Lindsay Kellogg
Vice President, Private Wealth Advisor
Goldman, Sachs & Co.
200 West Street
New York, NY 10282
United States
(212) 902-1000

From: Mindy Kaling
To: Sam Cook
Subject: cupid
Date: Fri, Sep 9, 2005

Dear Sam,

I know you said you're not coming to the party, *buuuuuuuut*:

My college friend Lindsay is coming and I promised her there would be single guys for her. She's really cute, *I swear*, and not in that way where only girls think it, like that time last year when I insisted Frida Kahlo was hotter than Britney Spears.

Love,
Mindy

Mindy Kaling
Latin Teacher, High School
The Dalton School
108 E 89th St, New York, NY 10128
(212) 555-1445 (work)
(617) 453-8688 (cell)
Tumblr: aromeofonesown.tumblr.com
AIM handle: LatinLover1979
—You can also catch me on Facebook—
"No more drama, no more drama." —Mary J. Blige

From: Sam Cook
To: Susan Cook-Velazquez
Subject: RE: RE: babysitting?
Date: Fri, Sep 9, 2005

Actually, I think I'm not going to go, so I don't need you to babysit. Thanks.

Sam Cook
US History, High School
Chair, History Department
The Dalton School
108 E 89th St, New York, NY 10128

SATURDAY

From: Mindy Kaling
To: Sam Cook
Subject: hi
Date: Sat, Sep 10, 2005 at 8:20 AM

Hi Sam,

I know you're probably out enjoying your weekend with your daughter, but I hadn't heard from you and I thought I would write anyway. You can ignore it if you want.

The truth is, I am having a pretty tough time right now. When Ethan broke up with me, I felt like I'd been pushed off a cliff. It sounds crazy, even to me, because now looking back at our relationship, I don't understand what was so great about it. I guess I'm the kind of person who likes to be part of something so much that I won't care if the something is bad. Then I went to Rome this summer by myself on the trip we planned together, thinking it would be like *Under the Tuscan Sun,* but it wasn't. I ate dinner every night alone at a restaurant where the reservation was made for two. I felt guilty that I was there alone, I bought two entrees, and ended up spending an enormous amount of money on food. Also, I got mugged the second day, which is why I'm wearing the same sweater in almost every picture on *aromeofonesown.tumblr.com.*

Now, there's a chance I *might* like a guy, I don't know him, but if there is even a remote possibility he thinks I'm attractive, I feel like I need to take that chance. Unfortunately he's coming with my friend Lindsay and the only way she'll come is if there are cute single guys there. If you could stop by tonight, it would mean so much to me. I will do anything for you, even stop sending you long, personal emails from this account.

Love,
Mindy

Mindy Kaling
Latin Teacher, High School
The Dalton School
108 E 89th St, New York, NY 10128
(212) 555-1445 (work)
(617) 453-8688 (cell)
Tumblr: aromeofonesown.tumblr.com
AIM handle: LatinLover1979
—You can also catch me on Facebook—

"No more drama, no more drama." —Mary J. Blige

From: Sam Cook
To: Mindy Kaling
Subject: RE: hi
Date: Sat, Sep 10, 2005

I'll see you tonight.

Sam Cook
US History, High School
Chair, History Department
The Dalton School
108 E 89th St, New York, NY 10128

From: Sam Cook
To: Susan Cook-Velazquez
Subject: RE: RE: RE: babysitting?
Date: Sat, Sep 10, 2005

Hey, remember how I said I wasn't going to go to that work thing? I'm gonna go. I will drop Molls off at 8 if that's okay. Will tell you about it later. xo

Sam Cook
US History, High School
Chair, History Department
The Dalton School
108 E 89th St, New York, NY 10128

From: Mindy Kaling
To: Sam Cook
Subject: RE: RE: hi
Date: Sat, Sep 10, 2005

OH MY GOD, THANK YOU THANK YOU THANK YOU, YOU ARE SO GREAT!

I'll never say US History is easy again just because it's only like two centuries old, and I'll never let anyone say anything mean about you EVER, like when people say you drink all the coffee but you never throw out the grounds!!

SAM!!!!!!!!!!!!!!!!!!

THANK YOU!!

Mindy Kaling
Latin Teacher, High School
The Dalton School
108 E 89th St, New York, NY 10128
(212) 555-1445 (work)
(617) 453-8688 (cell)
Tumblr: aromeofonesown.tumblr.com
AIM handle: LatinLover1979
—You can also catch me on Facebook—
"No more drama, no more drama." —Mary J. Blige

From: Mindy Kaling
To: All Faculty
Subject: EVENT REMINDER "A Back to School Soiree Chez Mindy"
Date: Sat, Sep 10, 2005

Hello everyone!

Tonight's the night! Just a friendly reminder, please allow 90–100 minutes to arrive from Manhattan if you are coming by subway. You can take the Q train until the last stop at Ditmars Blvd. Once you get out, you're on my street! I am nineteen blocks west on the right side of the street. I am sorry to say that because I live on the sixth floor and because it is a walk-up, the party is not easily wheelchair accessible. I have written my landlord about this matter but unfortunately it won't be resolved by tonight.

If you want to bring alcohol, that would be great!

Can't wait to see you there!

Love, Mindy

IF YOU CANNOT ATTEND THE PARTY FOR ANY REASON— PLEASE LET ME KNOW VIA EMAIL OR PHONE SO WE CAN PLAN ACCORDINGLY AND WE ARE NOT WAITING FOR A PERSON WHO ISN'T GOING TO COME.

Mindy Kaling
Latin Teacher, High School
The Dalton School
108 E 89th St, New York, NY 10128
(212) 555-1445 (work)
(617) 453-8688 (cell)
Tumblr: aromeofonesown.tumblr.com
AIM handle: LatinLover1979
—You can also catch me on Facebook—

"Don'tcha wish your girlfriend was hot like me?"
—Pussycat Dolls

10:23 PM   Mindy: Hey, Linds!
ETA on you and Seth?

I am saving the mac and cheese balls for when you guys arrive, and believe me, people have been asking about them.

10:45 PM   Mindy: Sam is here by the way

He looks pretty good
Better than I thought actually
You'll be happy!

11:12 PM **Mindy:** I had to serve the mac and cheese balls. There's still lots of booze left and I made blondies, the ones you like with no nuts. Really hope you're coming.

11:40 PM **Mindy:** Linds?

Lindsay: hey girl. 💀 11:45 PM

11:45 PM **Mindy:** Are you on your way?!

Lindsay: I'm so bummed. 11:45 PM

Lindsay: Still working

Lindsay: Seth took off with some of the guys to go to someplace on the LES where Ryan Reynolds is partial owner??? It was on Vulture I think

Lindsay: SO BUMMED

Lindsay: I didn't even have coke, so totally the worst. Haha

11:46 PM **Mindy:** . . .

11:47 PM **Mindy:** Oh. I get it.

Mindy: I hope you finish work soon. Thanks for texting.

Mindy: I think I'm gonna drink a lot tonight. I miss Ethan.

FOUR HOURS LATER

Mindy Kaling can't believe someone would steal a piñata from a party, is this New York City or Newark seriously
2:15 AM

Like · Comment · Share

Mindy Kaling had no idea that so many of her friends were from Newark. She apologizes, she is having a really bad night and like eleven drinks ok
2:18 AM

Like · Comment · Share

Mindy Kaling isn't sure why she bothers to throw a party anyway. Why even!? No one GIVES A DAMN ABOUT HER!!!!!!!!!!!!!!!!!
2:20 AM

Like · Comment · Share

Mindy Kaling is gonna start cleaning up this party. WHY ARE PEOPLE STILL HERE GET YOUR COATS AND GO
2:21 AM

Like · Comment · Share

Mindy Kaling SERIOUSLY WHO TOOK MY FUCKING PIÑATA??!?!?!??????
2:30 AM

Like · Comment · Share

TWENTY-FIVE MINUTES LATER

From: Sam Cook
To: Mindy Kaling
Subject:
Date: Sun, Sep 11, 2005 at 2:55 AM

I'm sorry I just kissed you.

Sam Cook
US History, High School
Chair, History Department
The Dalton School
108 E 89th St, New York, NY 10128

From: Sam Cook
To: Mindy Kaling
Subject:
Date: Sun, Sep 11, 2005 at 3:01 AM

It's just that, when I saw how upset you were that your friend's friend didn't show up, and that you, a grown woman, had pinned all your hopes on a stranger, it struck me as so silly and stupid. I mean, silly and stupid of me for being so happy about it . . . and then I just felt like I needed to kiss you, so I did that, and then I left because you looked horrified.

I should also note, I was and continue to be extremely, extremely drunk.

Please write back.

Sam

Sam Cook
US History, High School
Chair, History Department
The Dalton School
108 E 89th St, New York, NY 10128

3:14 AM   Sam: Hey, it's Sam

I hope this is your number and you get these texts

I have never texted before

I just want to clarify, when I said I was drunk it doesn't mean that kissing you was a mistake.

The opposite.

Unless you thought it was a mistake.

I know I will regret sending these in the morning.

SUNDAY

From: Mindy Kaling
To: Jim Dufault
Subject: Hello
Date: Sun, Sep 11, 2005 at 11:13 AM

Dear Big Jim,

I don't know how to tell you this, but, I just woke up, and while cleaning up my utterly trashed apartment, I noticed the unthinkable: two of the three trash cans you lent me are missing, presumably stolen.

You are not the only person who has suffered a loss—my piñata was also stolen, and yes, *after* it was stuffed with candy. It never occurred to me that someone would do something like this in my own home. Although, a lot of strange things happened last night, so perhaps it's just par for the course. First, a close friend didn't show up with a potential guy I might like. Then, while I was reeling from that disappointment, and picking up plastic cups from on top of my toilet tank cover (honestly, who leaves plastic cups in the bathroom of someone's *home*?), a man kissed me out of nowhere. It was pretty confusing because a week ago this man was someone I might have blocked on Facebook, if he was the type of person who had Facebook, which he isn't. Suffice it to say, I have a lot to think about, and I'll reimburse you for the trash cans, and please don't tell Headmistress Resnick-Klein. She has a PhD in being an old crone.

Yours truly,
Mindy

P.S. please don't repeat that old crone comment to anyone.

Mindy Kaling
Latin Teacher, High School
The Dalton School

108 E 89th St, New York, NY 10128
(212) 555-1445 (work)
(617) 453-8688 (cell)
Tumblr: aromeofonesown.tumblr.com
AIM handle: LatinLover1979
—You can also catch me on Facebook—
"Don'tcha wish your girlfriend was hot like me?"
—Pussycat Dolls

--- **Draft** ---

From: Sam Cook
To: Madeleine Resnick-Klein
Subject:
Date: Sun, Sep 11, 2005 at 2:37 PM

Dear Madeleine,

I am writing to offer my resignation. The reason being that I have done something to make another teacher feel uncomfortable, and I think it best that I

Sam Cook
US History, High School
Chair, History Department
The Dalton School
108 E 89th St, New York, NY 10128

--- **Draft** ---

From: Mindy Kaling
To: Sam Cook
Subject: RE:
Date: Sun, Sep 11 at 6:37 PM

I can't believe you kissed me. And it was such a good kiss. Like, *really* good. Like, where did you learn to kiss like that? You're so old! I can't picture you kissing a woman, only because you are so unpleasant most of the

Mindy Kaling
Latin Teacher, High School
The Dalton School
108 E 89th St, New York, NY 10128
(212) 555-1445 (work)
(617) 453-8688 (cell)
Tumblr: aromeofonesown.tumblr.com
AIM handle: LatinLover1979
—You can also catch me on Facebook—
"Don'tcha wish your girlfriend was hot like me?"
—Pussycat Dolls

7:02 PM   Mindy: Hey

Mindy: It's Mindy

Mindy: I was writing you an email but then I stopped.

Mindy: I'm upset.

Sam: I am so sorry.   7:03 PM

7:04 PM   Mindy: I'm upset because those email accounts are not for personal use, Sam.

Mindy: And I don't think this is professional.

Mindy: Do you?

Sam: No.   7:04 PM

Sam: It's definitely not professional.

Mindy: Then come over.

All the Opinions You Will Ever Need

UNLIKELY LEADING LADY

I WAS BEING INTERVIEWED AT A RESTAURANT for a flashy, nationally circulated magazine. It started out well enough. The journalist met me for brunch at a restaurant near my house. He then almost immediately began writing down everything I ate. This was a little odd because this wasn't a fitness or food magazine, but I didn't think too much of it. Maybe those kinds of details make the general public fall in love with you: "Ms. Kaling ate her omelet with a dedication I'm sure she applies to her career." I began to put jam on my toast.

"Not too careful with the calories, Mindy?" the journalist asked with a mischievous glint in his eye. I was taken aback.

Did he seriously just ask me that?

How do you answer such a question? Why would someone *ask* such a question? I mumbled something about liking jam and moved on. Later though, I couldn't stop thinking about it. Clearly what he meant when he said I wasn't "too careful with the calories" was: "Shouldn't you be more careful with the calories, Mindy?" I seriously doubt he would have said that to a slender woman. And there's no way he's saying that to a man. Because a man would respond: "Are you seriously writing down what I eat and, like, criticizing me about it? Fuck off, dude." The strangest part was the journalist didn't think this was a weird question. In fact, if you read the interview, he includes it in the article.

If that had been an isolated incident, I would've ignored it and filed it away in my mental file cabinet of "people who have bad manners and must have been raised by criminals."

But the thing is, he's not the only person who's interested.

I have a complicated relationship with my body. Or rather, I have a complicated relationship with my *stance* on my body. It is new and strange to me that I am now a person who has to have a "stance" on her body, since before I was on television I felt pretty detached from it. I thought of it as the vehicle that carried me to and from places my brain wants to go, like my car. In the past few years, however, I have found that people are preoccupied with it. So I decided I should try to reflect on it in some (hopefully smart) way.

Young women often approach me and excitedly tell me how much they appreciate the way I look. They like that I am not a skinny twig, because it shows that I refuse to change who I am and makes them feel like they don't have to either. I really love that.

But what they don't know is that I'm a big fat fraud. I'm completely *not* at peace with how I look. I don't wake up in the morning, look at my naked body in the mirror, and say, "Good morning, body. Once again, you've nailed it, you gorgeous imperfect thing. That wobbly patch of cellulite? A miracle. Each stretch mark? A Picasso. Holy crap, I look good! Who can I sext? Somebody else has got to see *this*!"

Most mornings, I wake up, rub the sleep out of my eyes, walk past the mirror, stop, and mutter, "Yikes," then quickly shuffle off to the shower.

I AM SO REAL

This is an example of the kind of thing that is most often said about me in the media:

"It's so refreshing that Mindy Kaling doesn't try to conform to any normal standards of beauty. She is just so real. I love that about her."

And my knee-jerk reaction is: *Wait! I don't want to be real! When I think of things that are "real" I think of income taxes and Putin's invasion of Ukraine. Real is bad! I want fantasy!*

My guiltiest example of this is: Once, at my dentist's office, I read a magazine article with the title "Curvy Celebs We Adore!" which featured a pretty photo of me. I loved it. Then I turned the page. The next bunch of photos were of actresses who were much bigger than me, probably weighing fifty to a hundred pounds more. My instantaneous reaction was, *Whoa, whoa, whoa. I'm not that big! They're kind of being liberal with the term "curvy," aren't they?* Then I really panicked: *I don't look like them, do I? I can buy my clothes at regular stores! I can still fit into one economy seat on a plane! These porkers would have to buy a row!* I was considering asking the dental receptionist her opinion on the matter when I came to my senses. I realized how absurd and gross I was to want a magazine to have stricter criteria for their empowering piece about non-skinny celebrities. I'm not proud of that moment, but sometimes I fall victim to my own insecurities. I never want to be part of the problem. I want to always be as body-positive as girls hope that I am. And yet I occasionally use the word *porkers*. I'm trying, guys.

I think the reason that such a big deal is made of how I look is that women who are my size are so rarely seen on TV and film.

Most women we see on-screen are either so thin that they're walking clavicles or so huge that their only scenes involve them breaking furniture and eating whole pies. There are exceptions, of course: my friend Lena Dunham, the wonderful Allison Tolman from *Fargo*, and . . . I sadly can't think of a third, even though it would be great to be able to list three here.

The conversation about me and my show is so frequently linked to the way I look that people who are deciding whether or not to watch my show must think subconsciously, *Oh, that's that show about body acceptance in chubby women,* because that's all they seem to hear about it. And my show is about so much more than that! It's about the struggles of a delusional Indian thirtysomething trying to scam on white dudes!

My deep dark secret is that I absolutely *do* try to conform to normal standards of beauty. I am just not remotely successful at it.

A VERY SCIENTIFIC ANALYSIS OF MY BRAIN

I can't for the life of me not eat something that I want to eat. You know how if you turned on a faucet in your sink to wash your hands, the idea of leaving the bathroom without turning it off is insane? That's how I am about ignoring delicious food. I can go five years without taking any kind of vacation, but I have never once refrained from eating a Girl Scout Tagalong cookie if someone brings in a box to work. The very *idea* of not taking one (OK, nine) seems crazy to me.

The truth is, if I were going to lose weight successfully, I would have to think about what I eat constantly. I cannot imagine a life more boring and a more time-consuming obsession than being preoccupied with watching what I eat. I mean, maybe being in a coma would be more boring, but at least then you're free to dream about all of your favorite foods. And the fact of the matter is, I don't have that much brain space to use thinking about it. Here's a diagram that shows what's usually on my mind:

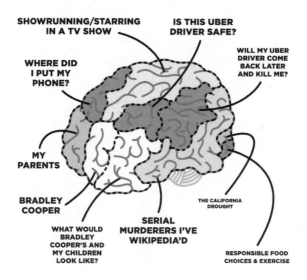

SHOWRUNNING/STARRING IN A TV SHOW

IS THIS UBER DRIVER SAFE?

WILL MY UBER DRIVER COME BACK LATER AND KILL ME?

WHERE DID I PUT MY PHONE?

MY PARENTS

BRADLEY COOPER

THE CALIFORNIA DROUGHT

WHAT WOULD BRADLEY COOPER'S AND MY CHILDREN LOOK LIKE?

SERIAL MURDERERS I'VE WIKIPEDIA'D

RESPONSIBLE FOOD CHOICES & EXERCISE

I suppose I could give up thinking about Bradley Cooper a little, in exchange for being ten pounds skinnier, but honestly: Who wants to do that? Would that even be possible? Did you see what he looked like in *Hangover 3*? Remember him in *Limitless*?

JUICE CLEANSES

Healthy people are always saying that diets shouldn't be diets; they should be thought of as "a new way of life." Well, that is just the worst thing I have ever heard. That's why I like crash diets like juicing.

Like everyone in Southern California, I've attempted several juice cleanses. If you live in the city of Los Angeles, it is your legal right to be able to purchase freshly squeezed kale juice from any gas station within a twenty-mile radius of the Hollywood sign. I did my first juice cleanse during the last week of 2012 as a sort of spiritual detox to prepare myself for 2013. I was a little weird then; I was watching a lot of OWN, and trying to be my best self.

In that week, I lost a full dress size. I only stopped because David Stassen, one of our writers, ordered French fries at lunch and couldn't finish them. He said, "I'm throwing these away. Does anyone want any?" In our writers' room, someone tossing a half-eaten container of French fries is like someone at a Wall Street IPO announcement party declaring that they were just going to throw away a bag of high-quality cocaine.* I lost my mind. I lunged at him and inhaled all of his fries standing up a foot away from the trash can. No food is as delicious as food you eat standing a foot away from a trash can. Ask any possum.

THE 21-DAY CLEANSE

That summer, encouraged by the relative success I'd had with my New Year's cleanse, I embarked on another one, but this one was for twenty-one days. You will not believe me, but I did not cheat once. I think I was only able to do this because of several highly motivating factors tied to my job. The first was that we were two months away from shooting season 2 of *The Mindy Project*, and it was written that I would appear in a bathing suit made of whipped cream, like in the classic film *Varsity Blues*. The second was that James Franco was going to be on the show and I was going to have to kiss him. Like every heterosexual woman and gay man in the country, I think James Franco is a very mysterious and sexy weirdo and I'd like to be invited to do a love scene with him in one of his art house movies. As you can see, the stakes could not have been higher!

....

* I've never been to one of these but I have seen *The Wolf of Wall Street* three times.

The first three days were terrible. The toughest part of juicing is that you are, well, constantly drinking juices. It's like an endless assignment of juices, with ten to twelve trips to the bathroom a day. And then, miraculously, on day four, just when I was about to eat the leftover candy canes I kept in a box of Christmas decorations in my shed, my hunger suddenly subsided, and I was in a loopy, great mood. The physical emptiness I remembered from my last cleanse was back! And it supplied me with a manic and infectious energy. I believed I was the funniest I'd ever been in my life. The downside was that I barely slept at night. I would just lie in my bed, grinding my teeth, waiting for dawn to break, like a demon in a music video.

I also began to have a pretty disturbing attitude toward eating. I developed a real superiority complex to people who ate actual food. I realized that this is how fashion editors at women's magazines must feel all the time. *Oh God, look at those sad piggos, munching away on their sandwiches.* I'd just sit there, sipping my kale juice, quietly judging everyone as they happily ate their lunches. And yes, maybe my mouth was full of saliva and the thought of putting an onion ring onto my tongue was almost sexual, but the point was, I was better than they were. I was juicing.

Costume fittings were, of course, the best. My jeans hung on me and everything looked so good. I could wear things I had long ruled out for myself, like jorts (jean shorts, duh) and midriff-showing tops. Basically I could dress like a slutty teenage hitchhiker and it felt great. But one thing was terrible: my social life was nonexistent.

I could not go anywhere or do anything. One Saturday night, an Internet multimillionaire named Eric (who was friends with some of my writers) was in town from Silicon Valley. For actresses in Hollywood, the "tech millionaire from Northern California" is a mythical creature. Actresses *love* tech guys. The idea is that we must seem glamorous to them because they are from some girl-less forest, and they are perfect for us because a) they're impossibly rich, b) they're nerds with probably not that many sexually transmitted diseases, and c) they have not been corrupted by godless Los Angeles, where if you're a guy with a car and health insurance, you don't have to settle down until you're sixty.

Eric was even better because he was a tech genius who made eye contact and didn't mumble when he talked. He was handsome and sweet and only a little boring. He had expressed to a mutual friend that he would love if I joined them for dinner. I was thrilled when I heard, and started scrambling to put together an outfit that made me seem like the classy Bay Area Trophy Wife I knew I could be. I could almost smell the musty interior of Alcatraz from the charity fund-raisers I'd throw there. Then I snapped out of it. I was two weeks deep into the cleanse. I was so proud of not messing up my spotless cleanse record by eating food or drinking alcohol, or even being tempted. I couldn't blow it now! Miserably, I told my friends I couldn't go because I wasn't feeling well.

The next day, I was kicking myself. What kind of juice-addled state was I in to choose swamp-colored grass water over hanging out with a cute, successful dude? Was a thin elixir of lemon and cayenne pepper going to marry me or impregnate me with two brilliant mathematicians/artists who would have his ability to write code and my style? Goddamn you, juice! Eric is probably married to a Victoria's Secret model by now or, at the very minimum, a Stanford physicist. That's when I decided: I will never cleanse again.

PERSONAL TRAINING

Like any good citizen, I've seen *The Biggest Loser*, so I know that increased muscle mass means a more toned appearance and burning more calories all day. But for years I just chose to never do any strength training because it seemed hard. It wasn't until a particularly disturbing night when I couldn't lift myself off the sofa because of lack of upper body strength that I decided it was time to see a trainer.

I'm going to be braggy for a second: I'm a pretty fun person to talk to. I find almost everyone fascinating and I love to ask questions. As a young teenager I was obsessed with small talk. Something about mastering it made me feel grown-up and like an "old soul." From ages twelve to seventeen, my poor parents were constantly having to listen to me prattle on about nothing, experimenting with chitchat. This quality has continued into adulthood, such that my friends sometimes call me a "talky-talky say-nothing." This side of me really gets turned on when I am with a personal trainer. I do it to get out of working out, obviously, but to the average personal trainer who doesn't get to interact with chatty comedy actors that much, I'm basically a sorceress. All they end up wanting to do is gossip with me and all I want to do is completely avoid having to do any exercise. Perfect, right?

This happened with my trainer, Joy. Every time she told me to get on the ground and do a bunch of burpees, I would distract us deftly. " 'Burpee' is such a *random* word. I wonder where it came from. I bet it has a really cool etymology; let's look it up!" I was like a snake charmer. Five minutes would go by while I was just lying on the ground, babbling. At a certain point I was so good at it that one day Joy arrived and I was like, "Should we just go get lunch instead of training today?" And she said, "Sure!" So we did. And then I realized that I had paid someone to have lunch with me, and I stopped seeing Joy.

MY COOKING IS BAD

In April of 2014 I made a resolution to cook all of the recipes in Gwyneth Paltrow's health-conscious cookbook, *It's All Good*, daily, for as long as it took to complete. It was my attempt to get in great shape, learn how to cook, and basically do a *Julie & Julia*, but with Gwyneth Paltrow so one day we could star in a movie about my experiences and eventually become best friends. It was also a way to improve myself that did not require going to spin class.

I decided to cook a salt-covered baked fish and green salad because it sounded easy and I could probably nap while it cooked. The first challenge was buying the ingredients. My entire day was devoted to tracking down branzino (a very fancy fish) and saffron (a very fancy spice) at various Southern California Whole Foods stores. Hell is Whole Foods on a Sunday. It's hordes of moms in lightweight fleeces pushing one another out of the way to get to bins of dry lentils.

The process of cooking my branzino was messy and difficult, and I went through about two rolls of paper towels. I found myself having to read the instructions over and over again. It was like my brain refused to retain the information because it was too bored by it, on principle. And once I had finally cooked my branzino and started to dive in, it hit me that cooking was not for me. In order to enjoy the *It's All Good* food, I needed to be living the *It's All Good* lifestyle. I was supposed to be eating my salt-covered branzino on a rustic outdoor table with witty dinner guests and my adorable little children bringing flowers to me straight from our English garden, like the photos in Gwyneth's book. It was not for eating solo while I sat cross-legged on the floor of my TV room watching *Access Hollywood* and folding my laundry.

In my heart, I believe that I am a passionate and intuitive cook who could make a five-course meal without even looking at a recipe. I feel I have the flash and charismatic personality of a famous chef, the fiery tenacity of Gordon Ramsay, and the soulful sexuality of Tom Colicchio. The problem is that I lack all basic skill. For instance, my dad had to come over to show me how to turn my oven on. It is sad when your hopes and your abilities do not line up.

I AM WHAT I AM (PLUS OR MINUS FIVE POUNDS)

I'm surprised when I remember that, physically, I resemble most women in this country. In the United States, a woman who is 5'4" and a size 10 is probably more common than virtually any other body type. But somehow when she is on-screen it's shocking to people, almost as shocking as seeing a married couple on TV where the man and woman are roughly the same age. If I were your doctor or your congresswoman or your sandwich artist, you wouldn't be shocked to see me, and yet, because I'm an actress, a grown man was amazed that I put jam on my toast.

Selfishly, I hope that after I write about it here, people will stop asking me so much about my weight. I can just say, "Hey, I talked about this. Go read the chapter in my book." If writers, even well-intentioned writers, stop focusing on that aspect of my appearance, it will become less exceptional, which would probably be good for body acceptance in women who look like me. Besides, there are so many other physical things about me to fixate on. My breasts are a little uneven. I have a scar in the shape of a swastika on my shoulder. That's nuts! And hey, I have character flaws too. This book is basically an exposé of them that I wrote myself! Focus on those! They're hopefully more interesting and funnier!

I want to say one last thing, and it's important. Though I am a generally happy person who feels comfortable in my skin, I do beat myself up because I am influenced by a societal pressure to be thin. All the time. I feel it the same way anybody who picks up a magazine and sees Keira Knightley's elegantly bony shoulder blades poking out of a backless dress does. I don't know if I've ever seen my shoulder blades once. Honestly, I'm dubious that any part of my body could be so sharp and firm as to be described as a "blade." I feel it when I wake up in the morning and try on every single pair of my jeans and everything looks bad and I just want to go back to sleep. But my secret is: even though I wish I could be thin, and that I could have the ease of lifestyle that I associate with being thin, I don't wish for it *with all of my heart*. Because my heart is reserved for way more important things.

I will leave you with one last piece of advice, which is: If you've got it, flaunt it. And if you don't got it? Flaunt it. 'Cause what are we even doing here if we're not flaunting it?

And that, my friends, shall go on my tombstone.

HARVARD LAW SCHOOL CLASS DAY SPEECH

*I*N FEBRUARY 2014, I RECEIVED A LETTER FROM THE CLASS *marshals of Harvard Law School asking me to speak at their Class Day. I know nothing about law except what I've seen on my favorite show,* Law & Order, *so basically I'm a legal genius.*

I was honored to be asked to speak at the school where, as a child, I had fantasized about breaking into their library. Here is what I said.

Good morning, everyone.

Graduates, parents, faculty. This is truly a remarkable day. For you, obviously, but also for me. After a life spent obsessing over true crime, the impossible happened: I was asked to speak at the Harvard Law School Class Day and accept an honorary legal degree!

Isn't that the American Dream? Me, Mindy Kaling, daughter of first-generation immigrants, accepting an honorary degree from the greatest university in the land . . . although looking around at this melting pot, there appear to be plenty of children of immigrants here. Hey, good parenting work, immigrants! Anyway, I am no longer just Mindy Kaling, actress and comedian; I'm Mindy Kaling, Esquire, attorney at law.

(A class marshal runs up to me and whispers in my ear. I listen and frown.)

Wait. What? Oh, I'm not getting an honorary degree? I'm just meant to give a funny speech and sit down quietly? OK. That hardly seems fair, but fine.

You're probably thinking: *Mindy Kaling? Why'd they ask her?* What does that triple threat know about the law? Sure, she's gorgeous in a totally down-to-earth kind of way. She's just a pretty Hollywood starlet. Yes, she was on *People* magazine's Most Beautiful People List this year (and also in 2008), but what intelligent remarks could she make about the law? She must be too busy doing shampoo commercials.

But I'm not too busy. In fact, I'd kill for a great shampoo campaign—if anyone from L'Oréal is watching this, Snapchat me immediately.

And I'll have you know, I know a ton about the law. I sue *everybody.* And excuse me, there's a burger named after me at Bartley's that they've guaranteed me is going to be there until another tertiary member of the cast of *The Office* gets their own TV show. And they don't just name them after anyone. Noted chef Guy Fieri has one. Noted drunk driver Justin Bieber has one. So, pretty good company.

Look, I get it. On the surface, it would appear that I'm an unconventional choice to speak here today. To be honest, I don't know much about the law. I graduated in 2001 from Dartmouth College, an academic institution located in lawless rural New Hampshire where, when you arrive, you are given a flask of moonshine and a box of fireworks and simply told: "Go to town." Only, there is no town; there is only a forest and a row of fraternity houses.

Actually, little-known fact: Dartmouth has a law school. It's just one semester and its coursework is entirely centered on how to beat a DUI. But I'm not here to extol the virtues of the Dartmouth Red Bull School of Law. I'm here to talk about you.

So even though I have no idea why I was asked to speak here today, I prepared for this speech very carefully, the way any good Dartmouth-educated student would: I drank a forty of Jägermeister, then called my dad to see if he could get me out of it. Dad said no. So I tried to hire a college freshman to write it for me in exchange for a $200 gift card to Newbury Comics. Not interested. Finally, seeing that I absolutely had to do this and couldn't get out of it, I rolled up my sleeves, sat down at my computer, and tried to buy a commencement address off of MovingCommencementSpeeches.com. My credit card was declined, so I wrote this thing myself, and here we are.

There are many distinguished speakers here today. I am sharing the stage with Preet Bharara, US attorney for the Southern District of New York.

In 2012, Mr. Bharara was named by *Time* as one of the 100 Most Influential People in the World. According to *Time*, he has battled terrorism, as evidenced by his conviction of the Times Square bomber. He's crippled international arms dealers and drug traffickers.

Clearly Harvard wanted you to see the full range of what India can produce. Mr. Bharara fights finance criminals and terrorism. I meet handsome men in cute and unusual ways on a TV show, and next season my character might get a pet puppy. Is one more important than the other? Who can say?

Dean Martha Minow is here. She has fought for women, families, and refugees, and is a champion for education. She has published over fifteen books, such as *Not Only for Myself: Identity, Politics, and Law*. Dean Minow and I have a lot in common. I too wrote a book. It's called *Is Everyone Hanging Out Without Me?* You can buy it right around the corner at Urban Outfitters, next to a novelty book called *The Stoner's Delight: Space Cakes, Pot Brownies, and Other Cannabis Creations*, and *Cat Hats: Sixteen Paper Hats to Put on Your Unsuspecting Kitty.*

But I digress. What I really want to say is that I am honored to be with such a spectacular gathering of very smart and dedicated people. This graduating class has three Rhodes scholars, eleven Fulbright scholars, and four members of the Peace Corps. This group before me is bristling with noble young people, many of you having already started charities and philanthropic organizations. And now, with this diploma in hand, most of you will go on to the noblest pursuits. Like helping a cable company acquire a telecom company. You will defend BP from birds. You will spend hours arguing that the well water was contaminated *before* the fracking occurred. One of you will sort out the details of my prenup. A dozen of you will help me with my acrimonious divorce. One of you will fall in love in the process. I'm talking to you, Noah Feldman.*

And let's be honest, Harvard Law is the best of all the Harvard graduate programs. The Business School is full of crooks, Divinity School is a bunch of weird virgins, School of Design is for European burnouts, and don't get me started on the Kennedy School. What kind of degree do you get there? Public policy? Right. You mean master's in boring me at a dinner party. The Med School is a bunch of nerdy Indians—hey, hey, hey! *I* can say that. Preet can say that. The rest of you? You are way out of line. How dare you.

But I digress. Again. I think I am just really excited to be here.

The real reason I am here is because I am obsessed with justice.

....

* To research this speech, I asked some law students for some prevailing campus-wide gossip. More than one person told me that all of the female law students were obsessed with Noah Feldman, a dashing professor who specialized in constitutional studies and who was also a recent divorcé. Dubious, I Googled him, and man, Noah Feldman is handsome. Believe the hype!

Not so much with the law, but with *justice*. Actually, law is that pesky thing that often gets in the way of justice. I believe in the Clint Eastwood school of law. An eye for an eye? That's absurd. It solves nothing. You take my eye? I take your *life*, in a duel, Aaron Burr–style. I don't want your stupid eye. For what? Yes, duels are the first thing you learn when you enter into my graduate program: The Harvard School of Vengeance.

But that's not what I wanted to talk about here. That's for the reception after.

The Harvard Law School crest has the word *veritas*, which means "truth" in Latin. I know this because though I have been known as Mindy all my life, my first name is Vera, which also means truth. That's true! Too boring to be made up.

I gesture up at the Harvard Law School crest, which looks like three bunches of asparagus.

And under these hallowed words? Three bunches of asparagus. Asparagus, the tallest and proudest of vegetables. The pillars of the vegetable kingdom. Like the law.

OK. That's not asparagus. I think that's wheat . . . ?

I give a big passive-aggressive sigh and begin rifling through pages of the speech.

OK, well, that's three pages of this speech. Nope, nope, that's a callback to the asparagus. I had a really funny run about hollandaise, that's out. You know what? This is not going anywhere. I'm going to move on from making sense of your crest, if that's OK with you.

Harvard Law has so many illustrious alumni. President Barack Obama attended Harvard Law . . . or so *he claims*. Elle Woods went here, from the trenchant documentary *Legally Blonde*. That's a very moving film. Dean Minow, you should check it out after you read my book.

Six of the nine Supreme Court Justices are graduates of Harvard

Law. The other three, I don't know where they went; I think University of Phoenix.

No, no, no. As we all know, they attended your friendly rival, Yale Law School.

OK, let's take a moment to talk about this rivalry.

I know you have a chip on your shoulder. Yale Law is always number one and you're always number two. Sometimes Stanford sneaks in there and bumps you down to number three. But let me tell you something, from where I stand, from an outsider's perspective: you are all nerds. The only difference is that you're the nerds who are going to make some serious bank. Which is why I'm here today. To marry the best-looking amongst you.

OK, back to your beautiful diploma, this Harvard Law Degree. It's not just a piece of a paper. You can do whatever you want now, and this institution will follow you everywhere. If you kill someone? You're the Harvard Law Murderer. If you're caught in a lewd act in a public restroom? You're the Harvard Law Pervert. And then you can represent yourself and you'll probably get acquitted because . . . you went to Harvard!

In fact, the only downside of this degree is later, when you run for Senate, you will have to distance yourself from it to seem more like a regular person. You'll tuck your flannel shirt into your freshly pressed jeans, and still this institution will haunt you. No matter how many diners you eat at, how many guitar solos you do with Rascal Flatts, you are Harvard to the grave. You won't be able to buy a pickup truck rusty enough to distance yourself from this place. Mitt Romney preferred to be known as "That Mormon Guy" to distract people from his Harvard past.

I am an American of Indian origin whose parents were raised in India, met in Africa, and immigrated to America, and now I am the star and creator of my own network television series. The continents traveled, the languages mastered, the standardized tests prepared for and taken, and the cultures navigated are amazing even to me. From Calcutta and Madras to Lagos to Boston to Los Angeles, my family, in two generations, made a dizzying journey, and the destination could only be America. My family's dreams about a future unfettered by the limitations imposed by "who you know" and dependent only on "what you know" was possible only in this beautiful land. Their romance with this country is more romantic than any romantic comedy I could ever write. And it's all because they believed that the concept of inherent fairness was still alive in Americans, that here in America they could aspire and succeed, and that their children could aspire and succeed to levels that could not have happened anywhere else in the world.

The fairness that my family and I have come to take for granted, that all Americans take for granted, is, in many ways, resting on your shoulders to uphold. You represent those who will affect change. And more than any of the others graduating this week from Harvard, what you decide to do with the next five to ten years of your life will affect the rights of people in this country in a fundamental way.

I'm now at the part of my speech where I am supposed to give you advice. I was wondering what advice I would have to give. Then I thought, You know what? Celebrities give too much advice. And people listen to it too much. In Hollywood, we all think we are sage advice givers and many of us have no education whatsoever. Actresses can become nutritionists, experts in baby care and environmental policy. Actors can become governors or high-ranking officials in religions made up sixty years ago! For two years I have played an obstetrician and gynecologist on a network TV show, and damned if I don't think I can deliver a baby.

So I was thinking, Well, then, who *should* be giving advice? And the answer is: people like *you*. You're better educated and you're going to be out there in the world, and people are going to do what you say, whether you're good or evil.

That probably scares you. Because some of you look really young. A couple of you are probably evil. To be honest, it scares me a little too. You look like tweens. This is ridiculous.

So be the people who give advice to celebrities, please.

You are entering a profession where, no matter what the crime, you *have* to defend the alleged perpetrator. Across the campus right now, Harvard Business School graduates are receiving diplomas, and you will need to defend them. For insider trading or possession of narcotics, or maybe both, if *The Wolf of Wall Street* is to be believed.

And most of all: it is you who are responsible for the language of justice. For the careful and precise wording in all those boring contracts I sign while I watch *Real Housewives*. You wrote the Terms and Conditions that I scroll through quickly when I download the update for Candy Crush. Terms and Conditions are the only thing keeping us from *The Purge*. I don't read them; I just hit "accept." iTunes may own my ovaries, for all I know. Meticulous research and careful wording is the gift you give to humanity.

"Employees Must Wash Their Hands Before Returning to Work." *A lawyer wrote that!*

"You have the right to remain silent. Anything you say can and will be used against you in a court of law." *A lawyer wrote that!*

"Mindy Kaling may not come within a thousand feet of Professor Noah Feldman." *A lawyer wrote that!*

These are the protections we take for granted. Like a medieval monk, you have analyzed every word, dissected every sentence, evaluated every statement for loopholes. Your dedication to tedium is astounding and admirable. You take words and turn them into the infrastructure that keeps our world stable.

The seductive Southern lawyers in John Grisham novels get all the glory. Your Noah Feldmans, if you will. But the rest of you form the foundation of our day-to-day lives. It's backbreaking and often there's not much glory in it, and, in that way, you will be the quiet heroes for our country.

However, those of you who are working for Big Pharma and Philip Morris—you will be loud antiheroes, and someone is certain to make an AMC series glamorizing you.

But basically, either way, you can't go wrong. I look at all of you and see America's future: attorneys, corporate lawyers, public prosecutors, judges, politicians, maybe even the president of the United States. Those are all positions of great influence. Understand that one day you will have the power to make a difference. Use it well.

Thank you, graduates; thank you, faculty, parents, and families; and thank you MovingCommencementSpeeches.com. Congratulations.

4 A.M. WORRIES

I SHOULD START OFF BY SAYING THAT I AM one of the only television writers I know who is not depressed. I'm not saying this to brag. God knows I have my own issues. For instance, I'm almost certain I suffer from undiagnosed cases of paranoia, irrational snacking, abrupt rage, and borderline clinical-level superficiality. I'm just bringing it up because depression is something that I've come to accept from my creative community and I realize that's probably alien to most people. I don't know why the funniest people I know are also depressed. In my mind I've romanticized it as the tragic price you pay to be gifted, like Mozart dying at thirty-five. It's sad that so many of my friends suffer this way.

I am grateful that I am a naturally cheerful person. That said, I am also a very anxious and high-strung person. Remember that kid who showed up forty-five minutes early to the SATs with eleven pencils and a huge black coffee? That was me. When I was a writer on season 1 of *The Office* I probably slept an average of three hours a night because I was so worried about being fired.

In my thirties, I gained a sense of calm that came from professional stability and, although this is not backed by science, a general slowing of my metabolism, which is why I can gain seven pounds from eating one heavy dinner. As calm as I might be, still, about once a month, I wake up at four a.m. and lie in the dark worrying about the same handful of things. I thought I would share them with you.

1. Did I leave my flat iron on?

2. Why was there so much hair in the shower drain? Am I going bald? Will I need to invest in a wig?

3. Where will I even keep my wigs? I have no room left! I keep shoes in my oven!

4. Why are my legs covered in small itchy bites? Do I have bed bugs? Do I not wash my sheets enough? Am I gross?

5. I have no idea if I am getting ripped off financially. I pay bills without reading any of the fine print. How much should a gas bill be? What does gas cost? Is gas the same as gasoline?

6. I am living beyond my means. Why did I buy that stupid photo at that charity auction? I'm not so rich that I can be buying photos! I don't even understand photography! I only bought it because I had wanted to seem classy and had two glasses of wine!

7. Do I have a drinking problem?

8. What if that young stranger who wrote me asking me to coffee to "pick my brain," and whom I declined because I was too busy, ends up being the next Alexander Payne and never forgives me?

9. When I watch movies and TV I am looking for things to dislike rather than things to like.

10. I will never have a husband and all my female acquaintances will.

11. I *will* have a husband and he will be like my female acquaintances' husbands.

12. What if I will never be one of the "greats"? What if I'm only one of the "fines"?

13. What if that commenter on the message boards who posts constantly that I'm an "ugly fat Indian girl who looks like a turd" is someone I know socially?

14. I am too cavalier about the crazy things I say out loud and someone will write about them in a tell-all.

15. I will never be famous enough for someone to write a tell-all about me.

16. People at work laugh at the things I say only because I pay them.

17. People at work don't laugh enough. Don't they know I'm paying them?!

18. What if I have an early-stage cancer that has not been detected?

19. Is my father lonely? Would he tell me if he was?

20. What if my kids are really young when I die because I waited too long to have them?

21. What if no one loves me except my blood relatives?

22. What if I forget the sound of my mother's voice?

23. What if God is not really out there?

24. What if I have nothing to say?

25. Do I have too much to say and not enough time?

They're awful fears. They're sweat-through-your-nightgown-into-your-sheets fears. I don't wish them on any of you. But if you have them too, that makes me feel better. And if you feel better knowing that I have them, I'm happy.

Then, miraculously, after agonizing in the dark, my eyelids get heavy, my body un-tenses, and a rolling wave of sleep passes over me. I fall asleep, my fears evaporating like the water in the humidifier by my bed.

WHY NOT ME?

ⱷ

ONE EVENING LAST YEAR, I WAS ON-stage at a Q&A in Manhattan hosted by a magazine to discuss my life and career. This was one of those fancy events where ticket prices are high, and there's wine and cheese beforehand, and cocktails, but no real meal is served at any point. It made you wish you had just shushed the naysayers and brought three hot little sliders in your clutch to nibble at opportune moments. No one else seemed to mind the lack of food, though, because the theater was packed, primarily with an older, mostly white crowd.

I was very tired. I had filmed a full week on the show, traveled on a red-eye from Los Angeles, done press all day, and arrived at the theater. It would be the last hurdle before I could go back to my hotel, take off my pants, and eat a room-service club sandwich while I watched syndicated reruns of *The Big Bang Theory*. Sheldon's sweet *bazinga!* would lull me to sleep, as is always my preference.

At the end of the interview, the moderator opened the floor to the audience. I noticed that the small group of people who lined up to ask me questions looked very different from the majority of the crowd. They were mostly young women of color. After a few people went, a young Indian girl stepped forward to take the microphone. She looked about fifteen, and not only out of place in that crowd but also a little young to be asking a question in front of such a big audience. I think she felt it, too, because I could see from the stage that she was shaking. After a moment of nervous silence, she asked, "Mindy, where do you get your confidence? Because I feel like I used to have it when I was younger but now I don't."

Context is so important. If this question had been asked by a white man, I might actually have been offended, because the subtext of it would have been completely different. When an adult white man asks me "Where do you get your confidence?" the tacit assumption behind it is: "Because you don't *look* like a person who should have any confidence. You're not white, you're not a man, and you're not thin or conventionally attractive. How were you able to overlook these obvious shortcomings to feel confident?"

But this wasn't coming from a white man. This was coming from a vulnerable young girl who thought that maybe, when I was her age, I too had faced similar obstacles. All she wanted was guidance, or maybe a little empathy.

My answer was not very good. My tiredness betrayed me, and I think I said something like: "Wow, I don't know. I think it's from my parents always telling me I could do anything. I wish I had a better answer for you." I wished her good luck, and she nodded politely and said thank you.

When I get asked the same question over and over for years, the words of my answer begin to lose their meaning, even for me. Talking about confidence has become, to me, like listening to the flight attendant go through the in-flight passenger safety announcements. I could be leafing through a copy of *American Way* as I speak. I open my mouth and glib phrases like "supportive parents" and "strong sense of self" leak out. People seem mollified, but who knows? Maybe they are tuning me out too.

As I watched her walk back to her seat, a wave of guilty regret hit me. This girl had done a lot to summon up the courage to ask a question, and she didn't even want anything in return other than my honest answer. She didn't want a selfie or for me to read her script, or to call her cousin's friend who loved *The Office* so she could tell me, "No, I loved *Office Space*. Were you in that?" She just wanted me to give her practical advice, and I answered in a way that was technically true but did not offer a lot of insight. And everyone had been fine with it.

And that really sucks. Because then why am I even speaking on panels in the first place?

So this essay is for that girl who went out of her way to be vulnerable in front of so many people, to whom I gave such a shitty, unhelpful response. Because I've thought about it now and I have my real answer. Hopefully she hasn't stopped liking me and moved on to Laverne Cox, though if she did, how could I blame her? She seems inspirational as hell and her legs are like whoa.

For the record, I, like everyone else, have had moments when I felt unattractive and stupid and unskilled. When I started at *The Office*, I had zero confidence. Whenever Greg Daniels came into the room to talk to our small group of writers, I was so nervous that I would raise and lower my chair involuntarily, like a tic. Finally, weeks in, writer Mike Schur put his hand on my arm and said, gently, "You have to stop." Years later I realized that the way I had felt during those first few months was correct. I didn't deserve to be confident yet. I happen to believe that no one inherently deserves anything, except basic human rights, and not to have to watch an ad before you watch a trailer on YouTube.

So here it is: Mindy Kaling's No Fail, Always Works, Secret

Guide to Confidence. This is why you spent your entire vacation reading this book instead of talking to your family.

Confidence is just entitlement. Entitlement has gotten a bad rap because it's used almost exclusively for the useless children of the rich, reality TV stars, and Conrad Hilton Jr., who gets kicked off an airplane for smoking pot in the lavatory and calling people peasants or whatever. But entitlement in and of itself isn't so bad. Entitlement is simply the belief that you deserve something. Which is great. The hard part is, you'd better make *sure* you deserve it. So, how did I make sure that I deserved it?

To answer that, I would like to quote from the Twitter bio of one of my favorite people, Kevin Hart. It reads:

My name is Kevin Hart and I WORK HARD!!! That pretty much sums me up!!! Everybody Wants To Be Famous But Nobody Wants To Do The Work!

HARD WORK; OR, THE THING NO ONE WANTS TO HEAR ABOUT

People talk about confidence without ever bringing up hard work. That's a mistake. I know I sound like some dour older spinster chambermaid on *Downton Abbey* who has never felt a man's touch and whose heart has turned to stone, but I don't understand how you could have self-confidence if you don't do the work.

I work a lot. Like, *a lot* a lot. I feel like I must have been watching TV as a kid and that cartoon parable about the industrious ants and the lazy grasshopper came on at a vital moment when my soft little brain was hardening, and the moral of it was imprinted on me. The result of which is that I'm usually hyper-prepared for whatever I set my mind to do, which makes me feel deserving of attention and professional success, when that's what I'm seeking.

I didn't always feel this way. When I was a kid, I thought I could cruise through life and get ahead on charm, like a little Indian Ferris Bueller. In the summer after fourth grade, my parents enrolled me in a two-week-long basketball camp. If it surprises you that a girl with my build was interested in basketball, it should. But I was, because I had a fantasy that I was in *Hang Time*. And I was terrible. I could've gotten better, but I didn't want to do drills. I just wanted to play pickup games, socialize, and drink Gatorade. I never wanted to practice. At the end of the two-week camp, I was no better at basketball. But at the farewell ceremony, trophies were handed out and I got one for "Coolest Clothes." I ran home, delighted, and placed it proudly on top of our TV for all to see.

Weeks later, I went to the TV room to find that it was gone. My beautiful trophy! Was it stolen by a gang of criminals jealous of my peach denim shorts from the Limited Too?! Mom told me she had "put it away." I didn't understand. Someone had singled me out for praise and the trophy deserved to be seen. Then my mom said something to me, slowly and carefully, like she always did to make sure I was really listening: "They gave you that trophy so you wouldn't feel bad, not because you deserved it. You should know the difference."

I was of course incredibly hurt and thought Mom was nuts. I thought, There's a great deal of value in being well dressed at basketball day camp. It keeps morale up and adds a sense of cheeky fun to the whole day. Later, I realized what she had said was true. A bunch of unearned trophies around the house would make me hooked on awards, which is bad in general, but especially bad if you don't deserve them. The whole experience made me want to win another trophy, but win it for actually doing something great.

Hard work is such a weird thing. As children and teenagers you are told it's a really good thing, but for adults it suddenly becomes the worst thing in the world.

We do a thing in America, which is to label people "workaholics" and tell them that work is ruining their lives. It's such a widespread opinion that it seems like the premise to every indie movie is "Workaholic mom comes home to find that her entire family hates her. It's not until she cuts back on work, smokes a little pot, and takes up ballroom dancing classes with her neglected husband that she realizes what is truly important in life. *Not* work." Working parents have now eclipsed shady Russian-esque operatives as America's most popular choice of movie villain. And to some degree, I understand why the trope exists. It probably resonates because most people in this country hate their jobs. The economies of entire countries like Turks and Caicos are banking on US citizens hating their jobs and wanting to get away from it all. And I understand that. But it's a confusing message for kids.

The reason I'm bringing this up is not to defend my status as someone who always works. (I swear I'm not that Tiger Mom lady! I don't think you need to play piano for eleven hours with no meals! Or only watch historical movies, then write reports on them for me to read and grade!) It's just that, the truth is, I have never, ever, ever met a highly confident and successful person who is not what a movie would call a "workaholic." We can't have it both ways, and children should know that.

Because confidence is like respect; you have to earn it.

THE TINIEST BIT OF BRAVERY

For those of you who would like to have *less* confidence, one way is to constantly read about how people think you suck. Or to hear people say stuff like "She's just not a star." And I hear that all the time. It's especially hard, when you hear these things every day, to want to keep putting yourself out there. People's reaction to me is sometimes "Uch, I just don't like her. I hate how she thinks she is so great." But it's not that I think I'm so great. I just don't hate myself. I do idiotic things all the time and I say crazy stuff I regret, but I don't let everything traumatize me. And the scary thing I have noticed is that some people really feel uncomfortable around women who don't hate themselves. So that's why you need to be a little bit brave.

People marvel that I am on TV because I don't look like other people who have been on TV. And to some degree, I get it. I like the way I look, but I'm not, like, someone you could see effectively playing Brookshelle LeFemme on *Pretty Lying Children* or whatever.

One of the unexpected and wonderfully fair things I have learned in my career is that if Hollywood were filled just with perfect-looking people, then soap operas would be the most-watched things in the world. But they're not. Looks are great, but they're not compelling enough. I've noticed that successful actors with long careers are usually talented actors with charismatic screen presences, and *all* of them must exude one thing: confidence. Yes, a lot of them are good-looking, but from my eleven years in Hollywood, I have learned a secret: "good-looking" by Hollywood standards is achievable by every human on the planet. Every average-looking American is just a treadmill and six laser hair removal sessions away from looking like Ryan Reynolds and Blake Lively (who are a great couple, by the way).

So that's what I think whenever I read something like: "How'd this chick get a job? I guess they're just giving away shows to every overweight minority woman who wants one now? Hahaha." So even though that hurts my feelings, I'm smart enough to realize, Oh, this poor dummy doesn't understand the way Hollywood works. Then I think of ways that I would beat him to death with my SAG Award.

Which is why you need the tiniest bit of bravery. People get scared when you try to do something, especially when it looks like you're succeeding. People do not get scared when you're failing. It calms them. That's why the show *Intervention* is a hit and everyone loves "worrying about" Amanda Bynes. But when you're winning, it makes them feel like they're losing or, worse yet, that maybe they should've tried to do something too, but now it's too late. And since they didn't, they want to stop you. You can't let them.

WE CAN DO IT! NO, I'M SERIOUS. WE REALLY CAN!

A general assumption about confidence is that women, particularly young women, will have very little of it, and girls will have zero of it. Just the attitude alone makes me sad: "We have to help our girls and teach them to be confident." Well, guess what, young girls. You aren't damsels in distress. You aren't hostages to the words of your peers. You aren't the victims that even your well-meaning teachers and advocates think you are.

We just assume boys will be confident, like how your parents assume you will brush your teeth every morning without checking in on you in the bathroom. With girls, that assumption flies out the window. Suddenly, your parents are standing in the bathroom with you, watching you brush your teeth with encouraging, worried expressions on their faces. *Sweetheart, you can do it! We know it's hard to brush your teeth! We love you!* Which must make girls think, Yikes. Is brushing your teeth a really hard and scary thing to do? I thought it was just putting toothpaste on a toothbrush. I get worried that telling girls how difficult it is to be confident implies a tacit expectation that girls *won't* be able to do it.

The good news is that, as a country, we are all about telling girls to be confident. It's our new national pastime. Every day I see Twitter posts, Instagram campaigns, and hashtags that say things like "We Will!" or "Girls Can!" or "Me Must, I Too!" on them. I think widespread, online displays of female self-confidence are good for people, especially men, to see. I just sometimes get the sneaking suspicion that corporations are co-opting "girl confidence" language to rally girls into buying body wash. Be careful.

So, if that girl from the panel is reading this, I would like to say to her: Hi, it's Mindy Kaling. I'm sorry I let you down. The thing is, I'm in my mid-thirties and I was wearing my Spanx for fourteen hours straight. You'll understand when you're older. Here's how I think you can get your confidence back, kid:

Work hard, know your shit, show your shit, and then feel entitled. Listen to no one except the two smartest and kindest adults you know, and that doesn't always mean your parents. If you do that, you will be fine. Now, excuse me, I need to lie down and watch Sheldon.

ACKNOWLEDGMENTS

I would like to thank: Jeremy Bronson, Lang Fisher, Dan Goor, Charlie Grandy, Robert Padnick, Julia Powell, Chris Schleicher, Michael Schur, Matt Selman, Matt Warburton, and Tracey Wigfield for their smart and funny thoughts and their friendship. Sonia Kharkar for her precision and for sitting next to me for months, eating cookies. Greg Daniels for his guidance and for his standing offer to take me hiking in Temescal Canyon, even though he knows I would rather die.

Ike Barinholtz and David Stassen for spending hours with me on dark stages, whispering hilarious and disgusting things.

Stephen Colbert, Barack Obama, Colin Firth, and Andy Serkis for our profound friendship (and for letting me use their likenesses).

P. J. Shapiro and Cliff Gilbert-Lurie for protecting me *and* being handsome, no small feat. Michelle Margolis, Alex Crotin, Katie Greenthal, and Amanda Silverman for their calm demeanor and hustle. Marissa Ross and Heather Morris for making it all so much easier. Sreela and Keith Ferguson for their loving affection.

Maya Mavjee and Molly Stern for their total support and patience. Suzanne O'Neill for her wonderful notes. Richard Abate for getting it. Bela Bajaria, Chris Sanagustin, and Ashley Chang for my lovely job, and NBC Studios, and legal for letting me use photographs.

B. J. Novak for knowing me better than anyone.

Howard Klein for always having the answer when I ask: "Oh, Howard, what's it all about?"

Jocelyn Leavitt for being there.

And Dad. For everything.

PHOTOGRAPHY CREDITS

Page 8: copyright ©Norman Jean Roy/trunkarchive.com (Mindy Kaling in *Vogue*); page 9: copyright © Bjarne Jonasson/trunkarchive.com (Mindy Kaling in *InStyle*); page 10: licensed by Warner Bros. Entertainment Inc. All Rights Reserved (Gollum); page 19: copyright © Universal Television, LLC (Mindy Kaling on *The Mindy Project*); page 51: courtesy of Julian Broad/Contour by Getty Images (Colin Firth); page 86: Copyright © NBCU Photo Bank via Getty Images/Justin Lubin/NBC (Mindy Kaling and Greg Daniels); page 91: courtesy of Fox Broadcasting Company (Mindy Kaling and Mark Duplass); page 92: copyright © Universal Television, LLC (Mindy Kaling and Anders Holm); page 94: copyright © Universal Television, LLC (Mindy Kaling and Seth Rogan); page 103: courtesy of Julia Powell (Mindy Kaling showering); page 105: courtesy of Fox Broadcasting Company (Mindy Kaling, Michael Spiller, and Tracey Wigfield); page 107: courtesy of Tracey Wigfield (Mindy Kaling with burger); page 110: courtesy of Fox Broadcasting Company (Mindy Kaling filming and photo of Mindy Kaling with Anders Holm); page 112: courtesy of Fox Broadcasting Company (Mindy Kaling at desk); page 123: *left*, Michael Loccisano/FilmMagic/Getty Images (Mindy Kaling and

ABOUT THE AUTHOR

Mindy Kaling is the creator and star of the critically acclaimed series *The Mindy Project*. Her first book, *Is Everyone Hanging Out With Me? (And Other Concerns)*, was featured on the *New York Times* Best Sellers list. She also starred as Kelly Kapoor on the Emmy-winning series *The Office* and wrote twenty-four episodes of the series, including "Niagara," which scored her an Emmy nomination. She has been named one of *Time* magazine's 100 Most Influential People. Kaling starred as Disgust in Pixar's *Inside Out* and made her film debut in Judd Apatow's *The 40-Year-Old Virgin*. She lives in New Hampshire and doesn't own a television.